ETHICAL DECISION MAKING IN ARCHITECTURE ● ÖMER AKIN

Cover Image

Mother Creator of All, The ubiquity of her Phrygian name *Matar*, suggest that she was a mediator between the "boundaries of the known and unknown": the civilized and the wild, the worlds of the living and the dead. Her association with hawks, lions, and the stone of the mountainous landscape of the Anatolian wilderness, seem to characterize her as mother of the land in its untrammeled natural state, with power to rule, moderate or soften its latent ferocity, and to control its potential threats to a settled, civilized life. Anatolian elites sought to harness her protective power to forms of ruler-cult; in *Lydia*, her cult had possible connections to the semi-legendary king *Midas*, as her sponsor, consort, or co-divinity. As protector of cities, or city states, she was sometimes shown wearing a *mural crown*, representing the city walls

Ethical Decision Making In
Architecture

Theories, Methods, Case Studies and Applied Ethics Anecdotes

Ömer Akin, PhD
Professor Emeritus of Architecture
Carnegie Mellon University
Pittsburgh, PA 15213
oa04@andrew.cmu.edu

ETHICAL DECISION MAKING IN ARCHITECTURE ● ÖMER AKIN

KINDLE @ CREATESPACE
4900 LACROSS RD
NORTH CHARLESTON, SC 29406

ISBN: 0-9762941-6-8

2018
© ALL RIGHTS RESERVED BY
OMER AKIN
ARCHITECTURAL DESIGN ASSOCIATES, LLC
+1 412 422 9805

This Title Is Dedicated To
Professor Emeritus Peter Madsen
Applied ethics expert

Peter Madsen is an award-winning educator, trainer, writer and producer of educational media in the field of applied ethics. He teaches courses in business, professional, computer, and environmental ethics in CMU's Department of Philosophy. Madsen also teaches graduate management ethics and ethics and public policy courses in CMU's Heinz College and at GESPIA, at the University of Pittsburgh. He is Visiting Professor at the American University of Paris where he teaches International Business Ethics.

Contents

Part I	**Theory: Ethics and Decision Making**
Chapter 1	Ethics: *Acting for the Greater Good*
Chapter 2	Institutional Ethics: *Professional Morality*
Chapter 3	Decision Making: *Exercising Choices*
Chapter 4	Design Expertise and *Creativity*

Part II	**Case Studies: Architectural Design**
Chapter 5	Sydney Opera House: *Risk vs. Innovation*
Chapter 6	Sydney Opera House: *Decision Making*
Chapter 7	Fallingwater is Falling: *Creativity*
Chapter 8	Crystal Palace: *Design Expertise*
Chapter 9	Pruitt-Igoe: *A Nation's Conscience*

Part III	**Methods: Ethics and Decision Making**
Chapter 10	Architectural Decision Making
Chapter 11	Plurality of Ethics Theories
Chapter 12	Risk-Cost-Benefit Analysis
Chapter 13	Project Management: *Planning*
Chapter 14	Design Optimization

Part IV   Case Studies: Engineering

Chapter 15   Citicorp Tower
Chapter 16   John Hancock Tower
Chapter 17   K.C. Hyatt Regency Hotel

Part V   Applied Ethics Anecdotes

Preface   *What is Applied Ethics?*
Episode 1   Air in Mainland China
Episode 2   Technology and Mental Health
Episode 3   What's with Industrial Farming?
Episode 4   Water, the Next Global Crisis
Episode 5   Funding Our Climate
Episode 6   A Tale of Revenge Gone Wrong
Episode 7   Lawyer Purchases a Box of Cigars

Citations and *Bibliography*

ETHICAL DECISION MAKING IN ARCHITECTURE ● ÖMER AKIN

Ethical Decision Making in Architecture
Part I
THEORY
Ethics and Decision Making

John Stuart Mill (1806 – 1873)

Part I Cover

John Stuart Mill (1806 –1873)

He was a British philosopher, political economist, and civil servant. One of the most influential thinkers in the history of *liberalism*, he contributed widely to social theory, political theory, and political economy.

Part I — Theory: *Ethics and Decision Making*

Chapter 1 — Ethics: *Acting for the Greater Good*

Chapter 2 — Institutional Ethics: *Professional Morality*

Chapter 3 — Decision Making: *Exercising Choices*

Chapter 4 — Design Expertise and *Creativity* [i]

National Nature Reserve, Yunnan Province, China,
Sketch by Ömer Akın

Chapter 1 Ethics: Acting for the Greater Good

Evident in their various dictionary definitions, the words, ethics and moral, signify closely related concepts, While they have been used interchangeably in some contexts they hold entirely different meanings. The word *moral,*[ii] a Latin term by origin, refers to *"characterized by excellence in what pertains to practice or conduct; right proper; dealing with establishing principles of right and wrong behavior."* Ethics is the study or morality.

Ethical is a broader term referring to the value of different kinds of life and activity; and moral refers more specifically to rules, obligations, and experiences. Even in their cryptic form, these definitions provide hints at some of the important issues covered under Philosophy of Morality (Williams, 1985). The use of the word excellence clearly alludes to individual virtues that underlie one of the original and remarkably resilient influences by Aristotle. The ubiquitous reference to the triplet, "character, actions and ends," recalls one of the well-accepted taxonomy of ethical theories (Williams, 1985).

Character is related to the venerable framework of Virtue Ethics where the virtuous characteristics of humans are the genesis and measure of its place in the moral milieu. *Actions* imply conduct that is sanctioned by rights and responsibilities with which we are compelled to act. *Ends* speak about the consequences of our actions that must add up to a net benefit towards the *greater good.*

Moral philosophy describes human conduct, both in terms of actions that are governed by these three frameworks. Most of us have an intuitive sense of what this means. We try not to lie or cheat; and under any circumstance not to maim or kill. We try to behave as responsible individuals and raise our children to be the same. The difficulty arises, when we try to understand what is meant by "responsible individuals." This is what Moral Philosophy tries to resolve, by describing the underlying principles of our actions and judgments; or resolving moral interests that happen to be in conflict.

Consider the following issues:

- As professionals, is it possible to adequately dispense of our ethical responsibilities by merely providing the *best* architectural products and services?

- Can we accept the broader interests of our *profession* to override professional *entities* legally organized into firms, and in turn, interests of these entities to override those of *individuals*?

- However highly regarded they may be, are specific professional acts moral, if they are aimed solely at elevating the personal stature of *individuals*?

It should be evident that the difficulty in answering these questions lies in the difficulty of agreeing upon a shared set of values and standards that differentiate moral from immoral, define priorities between conflicting interests, and enable the application of these principles by free-willed individuals.

In turn, these difficulties point to the ongoing discourse both on the principles themselves as well as on higher-level considerations that prioritize and organize the domain of such principles, or *Meta Ethics*.

Ethics: Morality of the Individual

Theories of ethics that attempt to resolve the dilemma of the individual versus the collective have been based on a handful of basic approaches. Some argue that through the application of a set of sound *principles*, the individual can insure a moral stance. Alternatively, others argue that the *intuition* of the individual is essential. By considering moral conclusions, including their conflicting outlooks, the individual can chose between them using his or her moral compass.

In Bernard Williams' chapter titled "Ethics" in the text titled *Philosophy* principal theories of morality are categorized into three sets. Based on fundamental ingredients of human actions and judgments, these are *virtues, consequences,* and *responsibilities* or *rights*, respectively (Grayling, 1995).

Virtue-based theories of morality: Aristotelian Ethics

This approach originates from Aristotle's theories about human virtues that can be traced back to Plato, and in turn to his teacher Socrates. According to Aristotle, human virtues, such as *justice, modesty, courage, self-control, prudence, generosity, benevolence,* and *duty,* determine ethical standards. These are the stuff of human character acquired through experience and displayed through action and emotional reaction.

This framework of virtues is motivated by the general belief that ethical behavior is what one expects from "good and decent" persons. Ironically, in Aristotle's historic model, slaves and women did not make the cut! As suggested by these exclusions, one can argue that this kind of virtue is based on cultural bias.

According to Williams, there are four reasons for being critical of Aristotelian Ethics: *grounds, content, unity,* and *reality*. First, the ground of the theory, based on genetic differences between actors, is fundamentally flawed. Second, the specific virtues cited are temporally biased. In Aristotle's original list "fairness" is expressed only in the form of "justice," "kindness" is nonexistent, and "truthfulness" is treated as a function of "boastfulness" or "modesty." Third, the dependence between many of these virtues, such as "justice" and "generosity," "courage" and "self-control," are all-or-nothing propositions. Fourth, the realism of such a theory is suspect since it relies on context dependence. "Generosity" in one context is not the same as in another and with judgments based on an individuals' appearance, which leads to stereotyping.

Today, Aristotelian theories have been revived through a movement called *Value Ethics*. In this case, virtue as the basis of morality is not due to the rightness of an individual's character, but due to the role his character plays in the wellbeing of others. Values derive from the flourishing of individuals; and through them we can infer judgments about actions that constitute the basis of morality.

Teleology: consequence-based theories of morality

Theories, broadly named *Teleological*, focus on the ethical results of actions and judgments. They have been dominated by a movement called *Utilitarianism* that deals with the estimation of the aggregate effects of all end results of actions. While the individual is capable of acting on behalf of a larger group or even society's "greater good;" first and foremost, he/she tends to look after their own benefit and that of those affected by these actions.

A central problem with this approach is that individuals act with limited knowledge of the consequences of their actions. Even if they could have perfect information, they would not be in a position to balance the diverse implications of these actions for others or society at large. Is the assumption that individuals will act in the interest of the greater good just naïve altruism? And ultimately, can we expect independent actors to arrive at the same conclusion about the greater good, with consistency? These are the problems related to the category of *norms*.

Other problems with this approach stem from the fact that utility of actions affecting some things of great value to individuals are not always measurable. How much environmental damage are we willing to subsidize when we sell or purchase any consumer product, including buildings? What harm would we suffer by not selling or purchasing these products? This signals the problem of *measurability*.

Finally, some technical difficulties also exist for Teleology. Is the collective utility simply equal to the sum of all individual utilities? Can justice prevail if the demands on individuals are not permitted to be equal either objectively or subjectively? This is the problem of *aggregation*.

Deontology: Rights-based theories of morality

Theories that are called Deontological are based on the concept of *nonfungibility* of agents' interests. That is to say, A's interests cannot be substitutable by those of B. A cannot do certain things to B, such as take B's life, even if this is in the interest of the collective. Also there are certain things that A is obligated to act on, on B's behalf, such as aiding in events of emergency or carrying out certain contractual obligations that cannot be ignored.

Many of our laws and religious beliefs attempt to govern through similar notions of conduct. Yet, conflicts arise due to the diverse rights of individuals. Without a notion of the greater good, it is difficult to manage the good of the individual. This is the problem of *autonomy of rights*. Opinions on the solution of this problem differ. Some hold the rights or the contractual principles sacrosanct, while others argue that such level of orthodoxy is tantamount to moral frivolity.

In an attempt to solve such problems, Immanuel Kant argued for the notion of "the kingdom of ends," which stipulates that everyone is obligated to laydown laws to benefit both themselves and others. In this way, we can expect convergence of these laws in a society of reasonable people. But then, such level of universal reason would in all likelihood render morality a foregone conclusion. Consequently, this approach reduces ethicists to become mere managers of self-fulfilling theories that are at best utopian. The question remains as to who has the moral upper hand when these laws are in conflict?

Are governments and religious organizations able to hold individuals in ethically good stead? Gauthier (1986) argues that individuals also have moral interests that go beyond their egotistical ends. Alternatively, John Rawls (1999) argues for the "veil of ignorance" that would distance individual interests from a contractual agreement thus making the greater good the principal motive of such actions. If one perceives their own interests to be served as well as those of others, even the egotistical individual would be compelled to look after the interest of others. Nevertheless, the problem of autonomy remains a difficulty to contend with, especially in *Applied Ethics* (Part V) where choices that need adjudication are in conflict.

Meta Ethics and the Morality of Institutions

Architecture is a field of practice. Like other such fields, in medicine, law, and education, it is subject to a full treatment of ethical considerations both in its practice and through the judgments it supports. Ethical theories that apply to the individual also apply to the institution of architecture. However there are important distinctions to be made in order to insure that individual's rights, as well as those of the institution are protected.

This raises several important questions. How can we balance the rights of the individuals who are members of a profession, against those of institutionalized entities, such as the American Institute of Architects (AIA), the Royal Architectural Institute of Canada (RAIC), or the Royal Institute of British Architects (RIBA)?

Who is accountable for these entities with life cycles a lot longer than those of individuals and offices? This introduces generational responsibilities that rarely exist among individuals.

Finally, institutions are prone to adopting formal policies and political positions that are persistently maintained, while those of individuals are not. How then can we mediate between the individual and the larger institutions and their politics? Published documents of the AIA should suffice to persuade us that there are special ethical dispensations allowed to institutions. Members and even non-member practitioners are urged to observe AIA's Code of Conduct, especially when this code is in conflict with personal rights of the practitioner.

For instance, after the 1980s, unable to maintain all of its sanctioned practices without appearing to violate anti-trust laws, the AIA was reluctant to sanction entrepreneurs who went so far as to bid at or below cost, just to be able to win a commission. Since then, the AIA has modified its stance; yet, debates about charges of anti-trust litigation and unfair price fixing continue.

In order to remedy at least the appearance of conflicts of interest between the architect, client and the contractor, the AIA had promoted an anti-design-build strategy. However, after re-considering the beneficial cost-benefit picture (Chapter 12) presented by design-build, individual practitioners and patrons, who have been the beneficiaries of such practices, were able to provide convincing evidence to support the re-sanctioning of design-build strategies.

It is not difficult to see how such policies can run against the principle of protecting individual members' freedoms. Some professionals do their best work in the design-build mode. Market conditions sometimes require that bids are lowered unreasonably in order to "keep an office going," and "allow free competition." If these conflicts are inevitable than what can we learn from a discussion of institutional ethics to manage *Meta Ethics* of architectural practice?

Gewirth (1984) makes the case for Professional as well as Institutional Ethics on the basis of three indispensable principles: *parity, hierarchy,* and *voluntarism.*

Parity requires that Institutional Ethics adhere to the same fundamental requirements that govern individual ethics: to promote and to protect the well-being and freedoms of its members. One cannot create a morally correct code of individual ethics without making sure that the institutions, just as individuals, are insured of freedom to act and to protect the well-being of all. Hence, the interests of individuals must be balanced against the interests of the institution.

To fines this point, a hierarchical relationship has been introduced between *infringement* and *violation* of one's rights, which mirrors the relationship between institutions and individuals. While remaining unassailable against outright violation, individuals, when they become members of an institution, automatically, if not voluntarily, agree to the possibility of infringement upon their rights. This is a principle of degree through which rights may be trampled upon while avoiding their violation.

Gewirth also emphasizes the principle of voluntary agreement of individuals with the edicts of institutions. He points out that without voluntary acceptance, codes of Institutional Ethics cannot be applied to individuals.

Conduct of Building Professionals

Before we focus on the ethics of the professional office and individuals who engage in its conduct, we need to better understand the genesis of architectural professions in the US. While counterparts in Europe and England were enjoying significant professional rewards, as early as in 1804; in the US, even during the first half of the 19th Century, there was no profession of architecture to speak of.[iii] The presence of professionalism in the US is a result of the alliance that was forged between architects of an artistic inclination, businessmen architects, contractors, developers and builders, at the expense of artisans and craftsmen Architects.

This has had a profound impact on the values held by architects even today. The primary agenda of an architectural commission is still characterized by the emphasis that is placed on the artistic and business aspects of practice. Even though there is sufficient diversity in practice, the charters of influential firms and institutions of higher education continue to emphasize a limited agenda: *shelter, activity, aesthetics,* and *economics*: one that closely resembles that of the early practitioners of the first half of the 19th Century.

A review of the evolution of the American architect's professional agenda is reserved for Chapter 10: Architectural Decision Making. Here we will consider how well this picture of political forces has helped shape the institutional makeup of the American architect.

First, we see that professional institutions in the US, while mindful of the fundamental freedoms and well-being of the individual, clearly emphasize preferences for a specific kind of professional. Architects are to be "artistic" beyond the call of duty. And by fiat, they are allied to sound business practices. AIA defines the responsibilities of the architect towards the client, as opposed to the contractor, as one of protecting the interests of the former.

In the hands of an unscrupulous contractor, a client naive in the area of technical matters, can be exploited both financially and along quality of product. The American Architect's job is to prevent this from happening. One of the important missions of the AIA Code of Conduct deals with organizing the hierarchy of relationships between interested parties and prioritizing their welfare.

It is worth noting that, in the US, registration as an architect or becoming a member of the AIA is a voluntary act. Of course this does not automatically make one's professional conduct morally right or wrong. After all, if you, as an architect, do not like an organization's code of conduct, you are free to join another organization or to form your own. In fact, there are organizations to which registered architects belong that present alternative options to membership in the AIA.

Acropolis, Athens, Sketch by Ömer Akın

Chapter 2 Institutional Ethics: Professional Morality

Ethical practice in architecture is the exercise of morally defensible actions and judgments; where moral is defined as, that which is "right" or "proper." What constitutes right or proper can be gleaned from two distinct sources: that which is right in the context of architecture and that which is right in the domain of the larger society within which architecture exists.

In the former case, we need to base our inferences on the historical facts pertaining to decision making in architecture (Chapter 10). In the latter case, we need to revisit the general theories of ethics within which those of the profession are subsumed – i.e., the topic or this Chapter.

Ethics According to Organizations

AIA regards the responsibilities of the architect as those that stem from obligations to the client and society. The first paragraph of the "Introduction"[v] to *The Architect's Responsibilities* by Murvin (1982) states that:

"The architect is responsible for imparting distinctive esthetic qualities to our buildings, yet his realm is not buildings alone. The proper fulfillment of the architect's responsibilities requires competent, ethical, and impartial service, not only on behalf of the client, but also in the public interest. Seldom does a building affect only its owner, nor does it stand alone.

For this reason, the architect is responsible for designing buildings that protect the health, safety and welfare of all who use them and also enhance the environment by taking due regard for the natural environment, existing physical factors, and circulatory patterns. In addition, the architect designs a building for efficient and economical operation and utilizes materials and equipment most appropriate for their particular application. In this way, our communities develop logically and intelligently; their architecture has a positive impact on society and is a source of satisfaction to the client and all who use it".

This is a clear indication of two categories of moral responsibility for the architect: one towards the client and the other towards society in general. The statement suggests both the end results that must be achieved, such as health safety and welfare; and the means with which these ends can be achieved. This includes competent, impartial service, taking due regard for the natural environment, and existing physical factors.

Thus mission statement of the AIA represents both Utilitarianism (*Teleology*) and rights-based philosophies (*Deontology*) of ethics theories. In fact, the latter is carried into much greater detail through dozens of contractual forms that AIA issues to regulate the fee structure, conduct and conclusions of the design delivery process. From time to time AIA also issues policy and guidelines to regulate all forms of rights and responsibilities including ethical ones.

Conspicuous with its absence from these documents is the *Virtue* based theory of ethics. There is no specification of individuals' characteristics and qualifications in order to exhibit moral conduct. This is an interesting position since early practitioners such as R. M. Hunt and R. Burnham, who have had tremendous influence on the inception of the AIA as an organization, were ardent proponents of the individuality of the architect. One explanation for this is that any attempt to define an *a priori* list of acceptable virtues could violate the goals of individuality.

Ethics According to Firms

While AIA represents the practice of architecture in national and international contexts, the conduct of architectural firms represents a great deal of independence from the rules and regulations of AIA. In fact the majority of licensed architects in the US are not members of AIA. Consequently, the ethical issues raised through the conduct of professionals are worth considering on their own right.

During the early part of the 19th Century, architects were, by and large, left to fend for themselves. Most of them were both designers and builders, leaving the client without any mechanism of protection from financial exploitation. In this form of practice there is no one with sufficient technical knowledge to shield the client and prevent unnecessary or incorrect construction practices.

In addition, conflict of interest in practice was not properly defined. Architects, such as Bulfinch in Boston, would purchase land based on the development plans prepared by his office or that of peers, thus benefiting from speculative land ownership. This kind of behavior was justified due to the absence of a professional fee structure and a code of conduct.

In a climate of mutual exploitation of the architect by the client, and *vice versa*, one was hard pressed to find reliable rules of conduct. In fact, the practice of owning the copyright for one's own design did not exist until recently. Builders, owners, and even architects used others' designs with impunity.

If there was any moral fiber holding the practice together, it was a form of self-imposed Utilitarianism based on the protection of the Greater Good. In the end designs were done, buildings were built, and architects and contractors made a living. It is difficult to say that these behaviors adhered to any moral code. As we shall see a little later, this form of practice has been a predictor of more recent developments.

Today we have principles governing conflicts of interest, fair-fee schedules, protection of design rights, and guidelines regulating the practice of design-build, alongside many other ethical standards, such as those encoded in building codes, and ordinances. These have been enforced by authority of a plethora of laws, bylaws, guidelines, and informal codes, either internal or external to the architectural firm.

Dana Cuff in her seminal work, *Architecture: The Story of Practice* (1992), cites several interesting examples. In the matter of jobs and the architect client relations she includes the following three examples that bring to the fore as many cogent points of view; such as the architect fighting in the trenches, ethics of Michael Graves, and that of Michelangelo.

ETHICAL DECISION MAKING IN ARCHITECTURE ● ÖMER AKIN

"It is fine to say you're going to do award-winning work, but you can't do it without a client. We're trying to do really good work when we get the chance. The trouble is, the only way to do better work is to have better clients, and the only way to get better client is to do the better work. WE only used to do development stuff -- all our clients were developers. Some of them are good you know ... Sometimes you have to admit the project is going to be a D-O-G. Then instead of pressing hard and putting in a lot of effort for little improvement, you get it out as fast as possible. Everybody designs a few dogs. It's inevitable. On each project, you just have to decide whether it is possible and worth it to do battle for something better."[vi]

This example displays the common plight of the architect based on no apparent code of conduct. The end result, that of keeping the office employed and the employees paid, appears to be the determining factors. These are the perceived obligations of the boss person. So long as the office is functioning to his/her satisfaction, they cannot deviate from the self-imposed edict to do better work. We see exactly the opposite in Graves' case. His conduct seems to be driven solely by the quality of work.

"We don't have a marketing plan at all, except to say yes or no to the things that come in. We have never gone out to get anything -- not because that was the plan, it's just that there hasn't been time to do that. If we get an RFP today in the mail, Karen will come to me and say "Do you want to go after a museum in Tucson? Here's the rap: you have to have a local architect, its $30 million, its schedule is that, you have to go for three meetings, you have to do this and that. Should we go after it?" I'll say yes or no. If that's a plan that's as serious as it gets...

It's not as frivolous as that because as the office gets older, and the people in it get older, we want them to stay desperately. [We] *want the office more or less as it is, with the kind of talent we've got. .. And if somebody makes X dollars with me and can get 2X across the street, I've got to make sure that the office makes enough money so that that person isn't going to make just 2X, but 2X plus something..."*[vii]

One suspects that this reversal of opinion by and large parallels the same in terms of Graves' fortunes, both literally and figuratively, as he is in the fortunate position of picking and choosing the jobs that come to him. One does not have to go far in Cuff's text to realize that there is no overriding moral principle at stake. When asked about his appearance in a magazine ad for shoes, for instance, Graves replies:

"For all the people who say 'You shouldn't have done it,' I have to tell you that it paid for my daughter's wedding. And, it's not immoral. Therefore, I'd do it again"[viii]

The true expression of the moral imperative in the matter of getting and holding a job can be found in Michelangelo's words to Cardinals as echoed in the give and take about the design of St. Peter's Cathedral:

"I neither am nor will be obliged to tell your lordship or any other person what I intend or ought to do for this work; your office is to procure money, and to take care that thieves do not get the same; the design for buildings you are to leave to my care,"[ix]

These examples illustrate different forms of obligation that the architect has to manage in the interest of clients, employees, and personal relations. However, as can be seen from the following quotes, management of a diverse set of obligations can become tricky.

Architect-1: *"A few years ago, I had a big job that fell through, so I borrowed money to make payroll when I should have let people go. Now I know you've got to be ruthless and make these tough decisions. I'd lay them off if it happened again. You can't get too people oriented or you'll lose your firm."*

Architect-2: *"I think you have to identify who you're willing to carry and who's expendable."*

Architect-3: *"But that will leave you with a top-heavy organization [because lower-level staff is most expendable], which is exactly wrong in a finical crisis."*

Architect-4: *"There's a big investment in every employee in terms of training them, so it's bad to lose them."*

Architect-2: *"But the cost of training differs, and draftsmen are very cheap."*

Architect-1: *"You've got to have a survival instinct.*

Architect-5: *"I did the same as* [Architect-1]. *Even though my staff knew I was borrowing money, when I finally had to let them go, they still didn't understand. I'd be tougher next time."*[x]

This is a good illustration of the interplay in the context of moral conduct based on the end result versus underlying principles. While Architect-1 and -5 realize the importance of hanging on to trained employees; they are not sold on the means of getting there, which involves borrowing money. While debating the merits of being principled, Architect-2 and -3 also realize the undesirable result of this approach, namely, creating a top heavy office, which would be to everyone's detriment.

In the following passage the obligation to balance one's personal life with professional responsibilities comes out loud and clear. The means for reaching a balance between obligations is not explicit but there is no question that it is a desirable goal.

"It was midnight, there were only twelve more hours before the project was due, and the studio was packed. It was the end of the first semester of architectural grad school. After a solid week of charetting this friend of my friend was nearly burnt out on beer, then coffee, and too many cigarettes. He had almost finished inking his drawings, which were really beautiful, when his wife walked in. He hadn't been home for days, and he was so bleary-eyed that he hardly recognized her. But she looked mad, and before he could say a word, she took his coffee cup and poured its remains over his drawing, and then she dumped the ashtray in the same place and ground the cigarette butts into the paper with her fist. All she said was, 'I want a divorce.'"[xi]

Finally in Cuff's work we find several passages that illustrate a rights-based approach to morality for architectural practice. In the first one, architects are discussing the rules of conduct in the office:

Founding Partner: One of our principal goals is to keep everyone in the office happy.

Partner-2: We discourage moonlighting, because it drains people from office work.

Associate: We never take calls during meetings with clients.

Partner-2: When someone [a potential employee] comes in to interview, we'd rather see loose sketches in their portfolios than hard lined, agonized sheets. Loose drawings, soft pencil drawings, have so much more personality and communicate so quickly with people. If I had my way, I'd take away all the 2H pencils -- I wouldn't even let them have pen and ink. "[xii]

There is an apparent effort to articulate the underlying rules that would lead to desired results; thus an attempt at a code of conduct based on Rights. However it is evident that what is driving the discourse is Utilitarianism. Similarly, in the following exchange between the fire consultant and a team of architects, the consultant is hard pressed to apply underlying rules of conduct without compromising the moral ground that loss of life may occur. Even in this case a Machiavellian approach wins over.

I thought you guys were different [from other architects] -- *that you were really trying to make this place work.* [After a bit of massaging by one of the architects] *If we're going to be safe, can we move this building a few feet away?* [But only a little while later, after making a concession, he returns to the moral imperative] *Now, how am I supposed to justify pulling burning bodies out of the building when you don't even have access roads?* [The architects assure him that they really need his help, and the fire consultant is the first to agree, Eventually he gives them advice about what can be slipped past the review panel, what can be pushed through, and what will never wash.] "[xiii]

The pattern is clear. Even though there is evidence that practicing architects feel compelled to come up with a Rights-based ethical approach, they rarely succeed. Their conscience seems to be overwhelmed by Utilitarianism. Once again, there is no evidence supporting the relevance of a Virtue-based ethics.

Practitioner's Ethics

Academics have been much more generous in describing the purposes of architects and architecture. This is not surprising since most of the treaties of the past and the present deal with normative descriptions. They talk more about the way things ought to be rather than the way they are. In a way this is perfectly suitable to the discussion of ethics since moral tenets are all about the way human conduct ought to be, rather than, is.

So, let's begin with the earliest of the architectural treaties: *Ten Books on Architecture.* Vitruvius text sees architecture as a human endeavor that gives expression to most basic human characteristics: *"the manual dexterity that distinguishes man from animals enabled him to construct shelters."*[xiv]

In accordance with early humanist philosophy, in many of the early writings about architecture, including those by Alberti and Ruskin, we find similar views on morality. Architecture, its specific forms, scales of buildings and architectural styles, are all considered on moral grounds.

There is also a prevailing discourse that anthropomorphizes architecture to the extent that its morality turns out to be a function of the virtues of the products of architecture. This is a rather curious deviation from the fundamental premise of ethical philosophy, which attributes morality exclusively to humans and not to inanimate objects.

The justification apparently lies in the belief that various manifestations of architectural objects, through their form, scale, and composition can represent human attributes such as Boastfulness, Modesty, Generosity, and so on.[xv] Such an approach represents the strongest evidence, yet, while not the only one, supporting a Virtue Ethics approach in the field of architecture.

This view interestingly enough has prevailed in the writings of many academicians who have studied various architectural styles and movements. Motivation for this approach, in most instances, is to find a theoretical basis for incorporating specific design styles in the design studio or high-style design circles.

One of the most remarkable treaties on architecture that deals with the Virtue Ethical attribution to inanimate objects, such as buildings, is Ruskin's *Seven Lamps of Architecture*. His contribution gave impetus to movements to follow, like Modernism. In his preamble he states:

"I believe architecture must be the beginning of arts, and that the others must follow her in their time and order: and I think the prosperity of our schools of painting and sculpture, in which no one will deny the life, though the heaths of many depend upon that of our architecture."[xvi]

This is a direct affirmation of the important role of architecture as the branch of the arts that connects aesthetics with the domain of ethics through the cultural context within which architecture exists.

His treatise puts forth a set of characteristics that architecture has to fulfill in order to meet its moral obligations. The seven lamps, "sacrifice, truth, power, beauty, life, memory, and obedience" are clearly driven from the Aristotelian notion of virtue. Ruskin anthropomorphizes architecture in the process of attributing these characteristic to it and not to their designers. This is in the tradition of early humanist philosophers and has been instrumental in passing on this approach to later generation ethicists.

In discussing the seven lamps of truth, for example, he begins his discourse by stating that *"There is a marked likeness between the virtues of man and the enlightenment of the globe."* Ruskin uses this metaphor to effect, which is pursued throughout his text to bolster the anthropomorphic approach. Later he speaks of the principle of truth as it applies to building design, as if the building's morality is exhibited in the inanimate objects from which it is made.[xvii]

"Architectural deceits are broadly to be considered under these three heads:1st The suggestion of a mode of structure or support, other than the true one; as in pendants of late Gothic roofs; 2nd The painting of surfaces to represent some other material than that of which they actually consist (as in the marbling of wood); 3rd The use of cast machine made ornaments of any kind."

Ruskin establishes a principle of moral imperative through each of his lamps. At once he is arguing for a Virtue-based ethic in architecture while also establishing principles like "Honesty," or 'Truthfulness," in the use of materials. This principle in particular became one of the flagships of the Modernist movement and has been hotly debated ever since.

In describing the Modernists, for instance, Royston Landau (1997) talks about several key ideas: Freedom from Convention, Social Responsibility, and, of course, Honesty of Expression of Materials. He points out that one of the basic tenets of Modernism has been the freedom from the "Tyranny" of classical architecture and its archaic patterns.

At once, his approach[xviii] harkens to the Aristotelian Virtue set and, at the same time, to the individualism of the early American architects. Landau also refers to one of the central premises of Modernism: the use of materials in a way that does not betray their natural qualities. Finally, he refers to the social and cultural context of architecture and reiterates the Modernist principle that requires the architect to be responsible towards the cultural context of buildings, if not their ecological environment.

ETHICAL DECISION MAKING IN ARCHITECTURE ● ÖMER AKIN

Thatch Houses in Xishuangbanna, Yunan Province
by Ömer Akın

Chapter 3 Decision Making: Exercising Choices

Decision Making is at once a cognitive act and also a field of investigation. The former is what humans do in order to go through their daily lives. The latter evokes references to at least half a dozen knowledge areas, like Economics, Management, and Psychology, and an even larger number of fields of professional practice, like Engineering, Medicine, Law, Business, and Architecture.

In this text, we consider Decision Making as a field of study that crosses disciplinary boundaries both through its generic definition as well as its shared methods of inquiry. We will start our considerations with the familiar, the everyday understanding of Decision Making by lay persons, and then move onto its exploration as a formal discipline.

In the course of a day, we are confronted with dozens of decision situations, some of which will rise to a level of importance that warrants cognitive effort. Should I drive to work? What kind of bread do I want in my sandwich? Should I take work home? What should I wear tonight? Ordinarily, we have no difficulty making such decisions and make them effectively. Each situation goes through a sequence of predictable steps.

First we consider the options before us; then assess their possible consequences; and finally, using some sort of metric, whether explicitly or implicitly, we select one of the options. Under this formulation, Decision Making is *"making reasoned choices, given alternative courses of action.*"[xix] Thus, the anatomy of a decision includes three indispensable ingredients: the alternatives, the means or methods of choosing between these alternatives, and the resulting choice of preference.

Without alternatives, no choice could be made. In such a case, it is irrelevant to speak of Decision Making. However, this is rarely the case since even while considering a simple action, say scratching one's head; we have the implicit alternative of not doing so. This characteristic, namely the null option or hypothesis, is trivial to deal with in simple cases, but becomes pivotal in more complex and critical decision situations. Failing to consider all alternatives and evaluating them explicitly can lead to decisions with undesirable consequences.[xx]

The same can be said about the methods of choosing and the final choice itself. Without explicit procedures for evaluating and comparing the consequences of each choice, we are liable to wind up with a kneejerk decision for the choice, which can lead to unhappy consequences. For instance, when choosing what to wear to an outdoor reception, we can end up being "eaten alive" by mosquitoes because the evening gown we chose is far too revealing or the cologne we're wearing is too attractive to flying insects. A poor Decision Making method carries the risk of leading to poor outcomes.

In everyday decisions, the three components of Decision Making, alternatives, methods and final choice(s), are often considered intuitively. We are accustomed to frequently making such decisions and these ingredients can be embedded in the *heuristics*[xxi] that we develop through commonsense knowledge gained from experience. Formal models of Decision Making, included in the subject matter of this book, however, cannot afford to treat these ingredients informally or implicitly.

A decision with any degree of potential impact on future results, such as business propositions, medical diagnoses, or design of building façades, get to be studied for days, weeks or months before they are finalized. While the ultimate decision can take only a brief amount of time to formulate, it is merely the tip of a much larger process that involves complex steps and multiple iterations. This complexity has provided the substance for the rich debate that has been raging, at least during the second half of the 20th century, aimed at precisely modeling and predicting human choice behavior.

What is deceptively absent from this discussion is the fact that there is nothing simple about cognitive processes that underlie Decision Making. The requisite abilities, such as long term knowledge, perceptual skills, cognitive strategies, and motor dexterity that the decision maker brings to bear on the situation, invariably take years to acquire and to master. Today, our understanding of Decision Making is the outcome of an intellectual engagement culminating in the question of how we formally represent and measure complex Decision Making behaviors.

In the following sections, as we review the emergence of this field and its methods and tools, we will underscore the importance of explicitly modeling decision alternatives, applicable methods, and the nature of final choices. Regardless of the fact that some choices making is mundane and others serious; it is important to note that the same cognitive processes are responsible for both.

Throughout its relatively short existence as a field of study, Decision Making has evolved from a mathematical model capable of estimating the dimensions of rational behavior to a complex model qualified by unpredictable and immeasurable components. The former, while precise, has been shown to fall short in terms of accuracy; and the latter, while presenting a closer approximation of human behavior, has been difficult to replicate under changing conditions. Further, these components are colored by a myriad of human behavioral tendencies.

Yet, the entire effort is science at its best: starting with a limited, rational view of the world and gathering, along the way, broad, descriptive constructs that embellish many research careers with numerous accolades and at least one Nobel Prize winner.[xxii]

Formal Models of Decision Making

Formalization of Decision Making theories has followed two distinct and related paths. These are known as;

- Normative Models
- Descriptive Models

Normative Models

Normative Models are involved with finding First Principles[xxiii] that underlie human choice behavior. Their aim is to describe these principles through formal methods, including mathematical ones that enable their application with precision to specific problems. One such approach to Decision Making that dominates the early debate in Economics is the "Rational Man" concept. In essence this concept holds that (1) people have preferred structures that obey certain axioms of "well-behavedness," (2) so that a mathematical representation of these preference structures can be rendered, and (3) choices can be modeled as maximizing an objective function, such as, "expected utility, subject to certain constraints."[xxiv]

Descriptive models, on the other hand, are based on the assumption that Decision Making is a result of the particulars of human cognitive processing and can be carried out through Stochastic Reasoning. This is based on the way humans "perceive, process, and evaluate probabilities of uncertain events." Furthermore, it is related to an Empiricist Philosophy and the Method of Induction.

For instance, research on 'intuitive statistics,' by Peterson *et.al.* (1968) led them to an optimistic view about the relationship between Normative and Descriptive views:

"man gambles well. He survives and prospers while using... fallible information to infer the states of his uncertain environment and to predict future events. Experiments that have compared human inferences with those of statistical man show that the normative model provides a good first approximation for a psychological theory of inference. Inferences made by subjects are influenced by appropriate variables in appropriate directions" [xxv]

The comparison provided by Peterson bears a resemblance to the comparison between Rationalist and Empiricist philosophies. This is not due to mere coincidence. Philosophical debate provides the foundation for this kind of distinction in a number of fields. Schoemaker, for example, makes a similar observation:

"This idealized conception of rational man has its roots in Greek Philosophy, in which an ideal person was viewed as someone leading 'a placid life amid external turmoil by the application of reason to conduct."[xxvi]

This dichotomy, while fundamental in the strategies and methods of Decision Making, is not manifested in absolute terms. As in the case of Classical Philosophy, the Normative/Rationalist and Descriptive/Empiricist positions are idealized models. Any given Decision Making approach may contain a combination of these two models. Methods considered to be in one camp may contain features of the other, at least implicitly, and vice versa. In the following quote, Feldman and Lindell (1990) drive this point home:

"Investigations in Rational Decision Making have frequently sought to contrast a normative model of Decision Making with a descriptive model. The distinction is somewhat misleading, since current normative models, especially SEU (Subjective Expected Utility), are implicitly descriptive. That is, the model is defined in terms of specific parameters (e.g., subjective probability and utility) and associated operations by which these parameters can be estimated (choices among lotteries, rating scales, etc.). By eliciting the appropriate judgments of likelihood and preference, the investigator describes an individual's decision-making process in terms of the parameters of the proposed normative model.

The resulting model can be said to be descriptive (of the person's state of mind) because it contains free parameters that have been elicited from the individual. In contrast, the earlier EV (Expected Value) model was unambiguously normative in the sense that its parameters were fixed (i.e., not estimated from the person) once the nature of the event system had been determined. In summary, the provision for subjective elements (utilities and subjective probabilities) by its very nature makes an SEU model descriptive rather than strictly normative."[xxvii]

It is against this background of give and take between Normative and Descriptive models that we must now consider each individually. For this reason our consideration should emphasize the similarities while sharpening the differences.

Normative Decisions of Von Newman - Morgenstern

From the lens of history as interdisciplinary as the topic of Decision Making has become, its beginnings are rather provincial. In Decision Theory, Normative Decision Making implies the selection of an alternative from among multiple, possible alternatives based on Economic Utility (EU), or some "value" convertible to Economic Utility, that is associated with each choice. Thus, the estimation of the EU of a selection is contingent on the attributes of alternatives under consideration.

Principles of this approach were first stated by von Neumann and Morgenstern (vN-MT), in 1947. In its axiomatic form this model underpins the Economic Theory of Games. As restricting as it is, it provides an excellent benchmark.[xxviii]

The underlying assumption of the vN-MT approach is that decision makers make the correct decisions about choices so long as they behave as "Rational Economic Men" or as modeled in mathematical terms. While this point of view has dominated the modeling of economic behavior for about a half century, modifications of this theory have been introduced from time to time in order to overcome the discrepancies between the predictions of these models and the actual behavior of decision makers.

All of these modifications were in an effort to recast the vN-MT in a more Descriptive light. This ultimately led to the recognition that Decision Making must take into account subjective assessments of utility and cannot be solely based on the assumption of rational behavior. This in turn gave rise to descriptive concepts, such as Bounded Rationality and Information Processing Theory.

Descriptive Models

Under this category, three kinds of theories have been developed by various schools of thought. The first one is those which try to diagnose the shortcomings of Normative models and suggest corrections that will take into account the non-rational behavior of human decision makers. These are called *Modified Normative* models.

The second one represents a radical departure from Normative models. It includes models in which the complexity of the Decision Making process employed by the decision maker, not to mention that their cognitive "mechanisms," would be considered as prerequisites. These are called *Information Processing* models.

The third category is similar to Information Processing in the sense that it treats Decision Making as a sequence of transformations based on heuristic rules of choice. These are called *Heuristic* or *Naturalistic Decision Making* models.

Modified Normative Models

While early experiments confirmed that vN-MT models were operational, somewhat later there appeared situations in which the behaviors of human decision makers systematically contradicted these models.[xxix] This led to the inclusion, in these models, of subjectively measured factors, such as utility and probability. Kahneman and Tversky (1979), in proposing such a modification, summarized the shortcomings of the classical normative models, through the concept of "decision biases," which include effects such as *Certainty, Reflection*, and *Isolation*.[xxx]

- *Certainty*. People generally do not weight the utilities of outcomes by their respective probabilities instead, they tend to overweight outcomes they consider certain relative to those they consider merely probable.
- *Reflection*. Individuals reverse their preferences, when a choice between two positive prospects is compared as opposed to a choice between two negative prospects,
- *Isolation*. To simplify their decisions, individuals disregard common components between alternatives, and focus on elements that distinguish them.

Information Processing Models

An obvious justification for human decision makers to exhibit non-rational behavior is not that they are incapable of behaving rationally but rather that they chose to behave irrationally under *some* circumstances. This is so because of excessive cognitive loads and psychological limitations that are imposed when we view the world strictly through the rationality textbook.

Under all conditions of conscious human existence, a certain amount of sensory information from the external world enters the human perceptual system that gets briefly stored in this system.[xxxi] During this interval, the perceptual system discovers patterns in the incoming information and attends to those patterns. There appear to be specific cognitive structures that enable the processing of this information. Newell and Simon (1972) offer a simple model to describe the anatomy of such systems (Figure 1).

First, sensory information from the external world gets translated into a symbolic code that is stored in the Short Term Memory (STM) system. This is temporary until the stored information is either incorporated in the Long Term Memory (LTM) system or discarded to make room for new information being admitted into the STM. Human LTM seems to provide both "unlimited" capacity for storage and a retrieval mechanism for ease of information access through recognition. The sequence of operations used to execute standard cognitive tasks is a stable, unchanging pattern for each human processor. Furthermore, the STM has a limited span to hold units of information, called *chunks*.[xxxii] Finally, transfer of information into and out of the LTM involves latencies in the order of five to ten seconds.[xxxiii]

Simon (1957) has persuasively argued that given these limitations, the ordinary Decision Making human cannot behave like the Rational Economic Man. He proposed an alternative concept called Bounded Rationality: *"...this holds that all intentional rational behavior occurs within constraints. Most decision rules that people use are sensible when viewed in the presence of these constraints... The theory of bounded rationality suggests that a distinction be made between subjective and objective rationality."*[xxxiv]

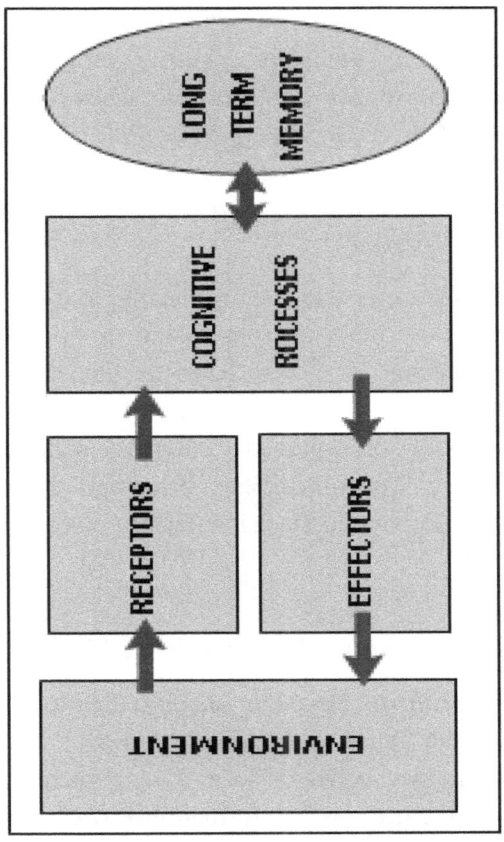

Figure 1: Information Processing Model by Newell and Simon (1972)

Simon (1957) has persuasively argued that given these limitations, the ordinary Decision Making human cannot behave like the Rational Economic Man. He proposed an alternative concept called Bounded Rationality: *"...this holds that all intendedly rational behavior occurs within constraints, including cognitive ones. Most decision rules that people use are sensible when viewed in the presence of these constraints, but not otherwise... The theory of bounded rationality suggests that a distinction be made between subjective rationality and objective rationality (as assumed in Economics)."*[xxxv]

People can behave rationally only within the constraints that heuristic processing provided by their cognitive systems:[xxxvi] These heuristic tendencies seem to condition the probability measures of classical Decision Making. Models of Bounded Rationality make allowances for cognitive functionalities, bringing the predictive capability of Economic Decision Theory closer to empirical observation.

Heuristics and Naturalistic Decision Making

Naturalistic Decision Making theories represent a shifting of the Decision Making paradigm.[xxxvii] Instead of comparing human behavior to a straw-man benchmark, or augmenting them through Information Processing structures and *ad hoc* Heuristic Rules, they seek new constructs, altogether. Cohen (1993) sees this distinction as:

"The naturalistic point of view involves more than simply looking for the same biases and heuristics in realistic settings. From the naturalistic perspective, an unquestioning acceptance of the relevance of classical normative standards

in untenable, because real-world decision makers appear to use qualitatively different types of cognitive processes representations... Formal models fail, not because people irrationally violate them .., but because the models themselves do not capture the adaptive characteristics of real-world behavior."

Owing to the ill-defined nature of architectural problems, *Architectural Decision Making* clearly falls into the category of Naturalistic Decision Making. We perhaps owe it to mere serendipity that latest achievements through the evolution of Decision Making theories happen to agree squarely with the nature of architectural problems. Both the context and the expertise of the architectural designer are critical factors in the Architectural Decision Making domain.[xxxviii]

Cacophony by Ömer Akin

Chapter 4 Design Expertise and Creativity

The commonly recognized *Aha!* Response[xxxix] refers to the moment when a creative flash arrives. Famous examples of this creative flash include the discovery of penicillin by Sir Alexander Fleming and the Greek mathematician and inventor Archimedes proclaiming *'Eureka!'* after formulating the theory of mass displacing its volume in liquids. While these anecdotes are, at best, exaggerations, they illustrate the phenomenon of the sudden onslaught of an idea, which is frequently experienced even under mundane circumstances: "why didn't I think of that before?"

If we examine other anecdotal yet better documented accounts of creativity we find a range of interesting issues to consider: Mozart speaks of the special qualities of the condition under which the creative "impulse" arrives.

"When I am, as it were, completely myself, entirely alone, and of good cheer - say traveling in a carriage, or walking after a good meal, or during the night when I cannot sleep; it is on such occasions that my ideas flow best and most abundantly. Whence and how they come, I know not; nor can I force them. Those pleasures that please me I retain in memory, and am accustomed, as I have been told, to hum them to myself. If I continue in this way it occurs to me how I may turn this or that morsel to account, so as to make a good dish of it, that is to say, agreeably to the rules of counterpoint, to the peculiarities of various instruments, etc."

Tchaikovsky, on the other hand, notes that the arrival of the creative impulse is sudden and unexpected.

"Generally speaking the germ of a future composition comes suddenly and unexpectedly. If the soil is ready -- that is to say, if the disposition for work is there -- it takes root with extraordinary force and rapidity, and shoots up through the earth, puts forth branches, leaves and, finally, blossoms."

Both of these accounts confirm, at one level, the *a priori* impressions we have of the creative process. Yet, they also suggest new insights. Tchaikovsky speaks of the "soil" being ready or the "disposition of the work" being there. Mozart speaks of retaining the memories of the pleasures that come and of mentally nurturing them into a "good dish." It is clear that what arrives and what happens to it next are related. There seems to be a readiness for the idea, which may be suddenly conceived. While we will not be able to fully explain a process as complex as creativity by relying on just these metaphors, it is reasonable to infer that what arises so suddenly does not arise from nothing but from the cognitive preparation that anticipates the idea.

Mozart, in fact speaks about turning the "morsel to account agreeable to the rules of counterpoint, instruments, etc..." There exists a body of rules that govern a creation. This is neither a surprise nor an obstacle to the composer. If these were not anticipated at the conception of the initial idea, would they have been recognized in such a matter of fact way? We believe not. In fact, we argue that the creative process is an integrated whole in which the conception of the idea influences and is influenced by the sudden occurrence of new developments.

Cognitive tools used in the development of the creative entity are also responsible for the inspiration that initiates the process. This preparedness for an important event is a characteristic of the cognitive skills possessed by experts.

When we describe the skill of an expert, whether it is in terms of an intellectual task or a manual one, such as driving a race car or playing the violin, we recognize them through the ability to handle the difficult with apparent ease, displaying a full command of the tools and knowledge required. While this is not sufficient to explain all that happens during the creative act, it is obvious that expertise is one of its ingredients. Without their musical expertise neither Tchaikovsky nor Mozart would have been able to develop their creative musical insights.

In formulating our investigation of creativity, then, we argue that the sudden onset of a creative insight, which has eluded the composer or designer until that particular moment, is a key step. There is no doubt that the soil upon which this Sudden Mental Insight (SMI) germinates has to be properly and painstakingly prepared. In the case of the expert this is a familiar yet laborious realization. But once it is complete, the conditions for the onset of the SMI are ready. Our approach to this question is inspired by our findings from other domains, especially the nine-dot problem,[xl] which tends to naturally elicit the SMI (Akın and Akın, 1996).

Based on these assumptions, we postulate that restructuring the design problem has something to do with expertise and the *"Aha!"* Response. Furthermore, it is related to breaking the *Frames of Reference* (FRs) in more challenging problem domains like designing a building's façade. To investigate this further we studied architectural design, musical composition, and puzzles that have the requisite attributes as challenging problems (Akın and Akın, 1996).

The Experiment

In the domain of architecture, we devised a simple sketch design problem, isomorphic to the Nine-Dot Puzzle.[xli] It involved the composition of a façade[xlii] for a given office suite floorplan containing five functions: a reception space, secretarial area, a conference room, a staff engineers' room and the chief engineer's room (Figure 2).

This problem is designed to have a normative set of design moves that are sufficient to solve it but is likely to yield standard designs. Such unsatisfactory solutions can be obtained by following directly from the information given and simply indicating four windows aligned with the marks on the floor plan (Figure 2). This façade is what is expected when the designers stay within the restricting Frames of Reference (FRs) of the problem. In this case, no cognitive insight is attained that goes beyond these FRs and the product ends up being routine. These designs are defined along four constraint categories:

o Size, proportion, location of the windows,
o Number of stories of the building,
o Construction of the wall, and
o Height of each floor. [1]

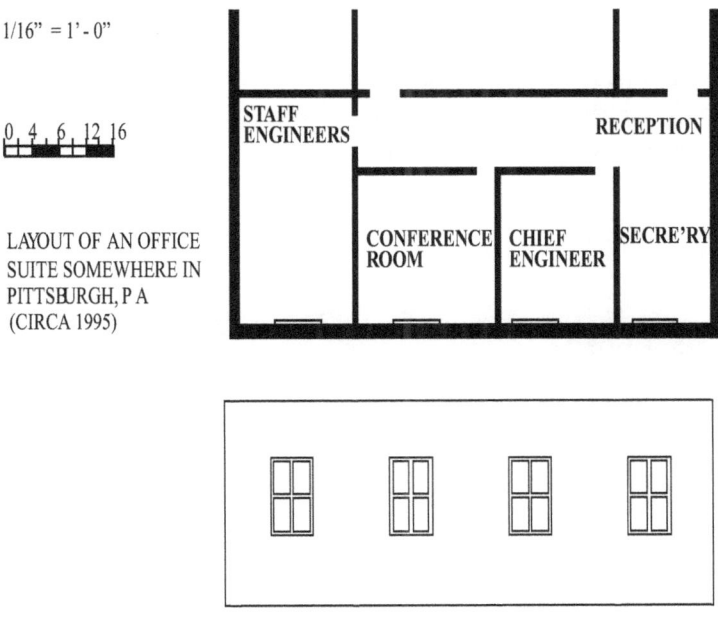

Figure 2 Plan and façade of design problem

Our hypothesis is that, unless these FRs are overwritten, a creative façade design cannot be obtained. In other words the *Aha!* Response leading to a novel design solution liberates the solution domain from imposition of the given FRs. Realizing the creative breakthrough should involve both the didactic principle of the insight (the need to go beyond each restricting FR) and the procedural knowledge needed to establish new FRs; such as, misaligning the windows, extending the eaves, and altering the massing of the façade (Figure 3).

The items in list [1] constitute a set of features that can be used to suggest possible design insights. In addition, certain designerly strategies may be instrumental in actually initiating these insights. Clearly, the expert designer will be more likely to use such strategies.

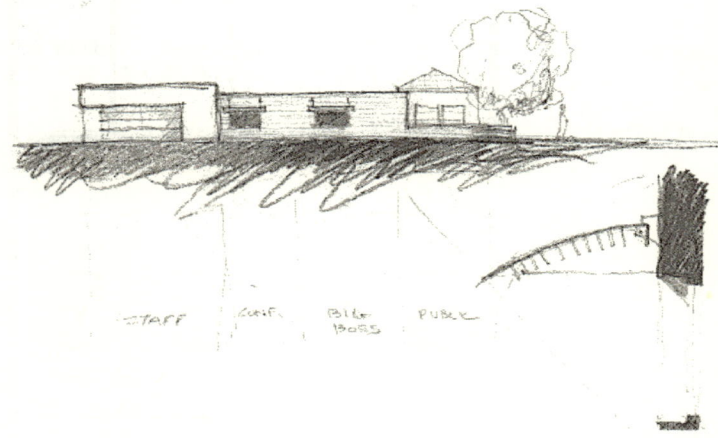

Figure 3 Façade design by expert designer

Figure 4 Façade design by novice designer

Formulated in this way, the design insight is expected to function as a trigger for creativity. Furthermore, externally supplied hints cover only a part of the knowledge needed to construct new FRs.

A video camera was used to record both the motor and verbal protocols of eight subjects. Upon completion of the design task, the subjects were given a brief questionnaire about the FR categories included in [1]. These *protocols*[xliii] were transcribed and segmented by two independent experimenters using verification techniques recommended for Protocol Analysis (Ericsson and Simon, 1993). The analysis examined the FRs used by all eight subjects. Some of these FRs were inferred from the experiment's instructions. The subjects also developed new ones.

Our analysis was intended to validate our hypotheses about design insights and FRs in the sketch design problem and identify which strategies were used by the subjects. This was accomplished in three steps:

1. identify the FRs used in defining the design strategy,
2. identify the breakouts from these FRs, and
3. show how these breakouts correspond to design insights.

In reporting our results we restricted our observations to two subjects: Subject-1: a designer (Figure 3) and Subject-2: a non-designer (Figure 4). In Subject-1's protocol data, six FRs were identified. In the second column of Table 1, the first number following the letters "FR" designates the subject, the next number after the hyphen is the FRs id number, and the numbers following the period, if any, identify versions of the FR.

The first FR from which both subjects tried to breakout is the regularity imposed by the windows (Tables 1 and 2). This is not surprising since façade design, more often than not, hinges upon the placement and proportions of windows. In the case of Subject-1, he referred to the existing window geometry as "repetitive" and "deadening" (Table1, FR1-1). He spoke about specific design operations such as infusing "variety," "hierarchy" and various "grouping" strategies, in order to fix this design feature.

Subject-1 also relied on creating bookends, a well-known principle of two-dimensional composition. This principle is based on the specialization through variations in size, shape or position, of the windows occupying the extreme positions of the façade. Such an arrangement can help complement and add variety to the repetitive pattern of the window patterns, act as terminal features on the two extreme positions, far left and far right.

This move had the effect of freeing Subject-1 to experiment with patterns that are not necessarily in conformance with the floor plan. The result turns out to be, as it should when the bookends principle is properly applied, as an enhancement (Figure 3).

This effect can be observed in some of the other features of this design, such as, the roof form, selection of materials, and solar shading devices. By balancing the asymmetrical roof forms on the opposing ends of the building, Subject-1 emphasizes the special position of the two ends of the façade. The "eyebrow" like forms placed above the middle windows are shading devices (Figure 3), and they also help bridge the differences between the middle of the façade and the windows at the two ends.

Table 1: Frames of Reference of Subject-1

	Frame of Reference	Source	Reference
FR1-1	window geometry	given plan	"repeated windows"
FR1-2	ceiling height	assumed standard	"12 ft. ceiling height"
FR1-3.1	being located at ground floor	statement	"on ground floor"
FR 1-3.2	part of a single story building	implicit assumption	see FR1-3.1
FR1-4	relief from the planar surfaces	implicit assumption	".. which gives some relief"
FR1-5	materials used on facade	implicit assumption	"texture, contrast to material"

In the case of Subject-2 (Table 2), four FRs were observed and only three of them were broken out of. The juxtaposition of their steel construction against the heavy, earthy textures of the brick wall provides a promising design theme for the selection of construction materials. These FRs happen to be proper subsets of some of the others that have been broken out of by Subject-1.

The designs produced by these two subjects, however, are significantly different. Note, for instance, how the non-designer's solution (Figure 4) is anticipated by the normative solution (Figure 2) as opposed to how different the designer's solution (Figure 3) turned out to be.

Upon closer examination of Tables 1 and 2, it appears that the manner in which the two subjects broke out of their FRs are indeed very different. The window patterns are the very first FRs from which Subject-2 tries to break out. She remarks "I mean if you're looking in, I don't know that I would necessarily see anything. If I stand outside all I pretty much see is windows... right?" However, the features used to achieve this break out are standard features found in "normal" house images. The roof is a simple gable, the walls are brick, and the windows are regularly spaced.

Table 2: Frames of Reference of Subject-2

ID	Frame of Reference	Source	Reference
FR2-1	size of windows	given plan	"want to make [these] window[s] bigger"
FR2-2	access door	given plan	"don't see any doors"
FR2-3	ceiling and roof form	statement	"nice big curvy ceiling-like roof"
FR2-4	material selection	statement	"maybe [the wall] could be brick"

The only two aspects different from the standard image are the entrance for which Subject-2 decides (Table 2, FR2.2) and the chimney, which is not included in her drawing. Once again, in conformance with the idealized house image, the materials selected are brick and shingles. In fact, in her protocol, Subject-2 refers to it as part of her childhood model-building activity.

While Subject-2's solution represents the standard solution to the problem – preserving the entire set of FRs provided by the problem statement with the exception of lowered sill heights – Subject-1 creates a novel façade with unique features. He also develops a formal hierarchy and integration of forms and materials.

These differences point to the same phenomenon observed in puzzles, that is, recognizing that the need to breakout of FRs not being sufficient to reach a creative solution (Akın and Akın, 1996). In addition to breaking out of FRs one needs to develop new procedural knowledge in order to actually implement each novel break out move.

In the case of Subject-2, due to a lack of training in architectural design, this procedural knowledge appears to be lacking. She does not have the technical and experiential background. On the other hand, Subject-1 is trained to have the skills to assemble façade compositions, spatial compositions, sun shading devices, and construction details.

Another important difference is the representations used by designers. While designers participating in our experiment drew sections of the façade to explore the thickness of materials and construction details; none of the non-designers did so. Except for one non-designer, no other one had training in drafting or architectural design.

In design of buildings, as is the case with other areas of artistic composition, redefining the problem space is a critical aspect of creativity. Unless the designer is able to shift into the exploration of a new Frame of Reference Space, he/she is bound to get stuck with continuously bumping into the Restricting Frames of the problem. Similar strategies might explain how ground breaking paintings, sculpture, musical compositions come about.

However intuitive the process might turn out to be in the case of specific individuals, it would be difficult to explain the genius of Caravaggio's choice of subjects, Van Gogh's colors or Picasso's abstractions without speaking about brand new Frames of Reference they have created in contradistinction to those commonly used in preceding periods and styles; like High Renaissance, Impressionism, and Modernism.

The conventional approach to identifying these creative breakthroughs has been the use of indirect means such as finding outliers or the *Aha!* Response. As observed in puzzles, inventions and designs,[xliv] the knowledge of the creative agent plays a key role in their achievements. Once again, it is important to underscore that the *Aha!* response is related to but not an essential part of creative acts. It seems to be more important for the socio-psychological aspects of discoveries and creative inventions, than for the cognitive psychology of creativity.

Expertise in Felds Other Than Architecture

Since the early works of deGroot (1965) there has been considerable development in the methods used to measure chess masters' expertise and the calibration of their skills. Others (Chase and Simon, 1973) have also explored theories about the perceptual and cognitive skills that are necessary in chess. One of the most remarkable findings of these works is that factors which mark expertise in chess have less to do with the ability to search new move possibilities and more with the ability to recognize patterns.

While determining their moves, chess masters do not display superiority in looking ahead many more plies than non-experts. Instead, they display an uncanny ability to see relationships on the chess board, which are not apparent to less experienced players.

This general result has been responsible for directing studies of expertise to the domain of memory and recognition, particularly of *chunks* of information useful in problem solving (Miller, 1956); and unrelated to solution-search behavior.

The Time-at-Task Hypothesis, which underlies these studies, states that to become an expert in a given field one needs to acquire a large number of chunks. Generally, this is in the order of 100,000. Furthermore, the minimum amount of time required to gain this knowledge is considered to be a decade. Principally, Hayes has conducted studies to verify this hypothesis in several areas.

Hayes' work on musical composition (1982) is based on surveys of all notable classical composers culled from publications such as the *Schwann's Guide*. He has considered two key questions. When did a particular composer start musical training? When did the compositions by the composer reach the maturity that is normally associated with mastery that is associated with expertise?

In answering the first question, he found adequate data in biographical sources. In most cases the composers started training formally or experienced some incident revealing their prodigious careers. These were unambiguous events indicating the beginning of their musical training. In answering the second question, he found evidence in several independent sources to confirm results; such as, the issuing of recordings of works listed in *Schwann's Guide* (August 1979) and other publications like it. In other cases, published opinions of authoritative musical historians were consulted (Figure 5).

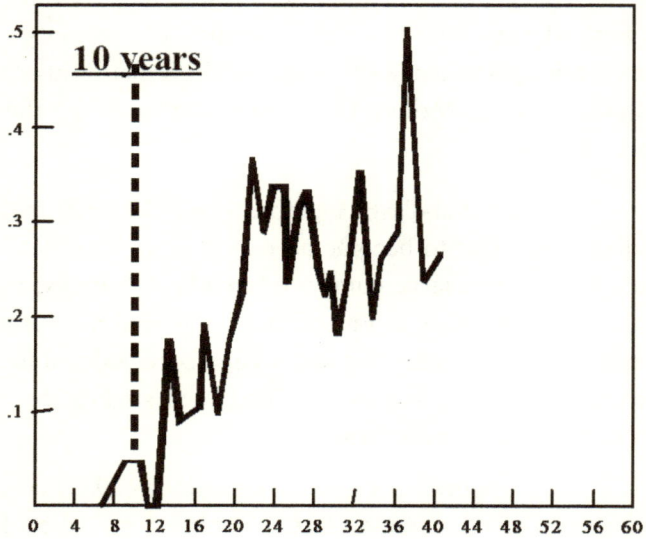

Figure 5 Time at task for music masters

Mozart was one of the first composers who were studied largely because of the commonly accepted notion that his development as a composer was most likely to present the strongest counter example to the Time-at-Task Hypothesis. Surprisingly, Mozart's case confirmed the hypothesis, just as the data on a large number of other composers (Figure 5). Yet it was observed that the hypothesis was a necessary but insufficient factor in the emergence of expertise.

Each of the top 40 musicians, including musical prodigies, spent a minimum of ten years at task before they become experts. The only exception to this was Robert Schumann, who did it in nine years. This is not an argument for a "magical" number, rather one of natural development.

That is what we generally consider through consensus to identify "expert" performance. Hence, there is some arbitrariness in this measure to the extent that there is in our notion of expertise. Furthermore, Hayes' results are silent when it comes to special aptitude or talent. There is nothing that either necessitates or refutes the possible role of talent that is beyond those implied by the limitations of a minimum of ten years at task.

Similar results have been found in the fields of painting and poetry (Hayes, 1982). Determination of expertise in the case of poetry and the beginning of training in the case of both poetry and painting were problematic. Researchers were able to develop specific methods for overcoming these difficulties and to show results similar to those in the area of musical composition.

Ethical Decision Making in Architecture — Ömer Akin

Ethical Decision Making in Architecture

Part II
Case Studies:
Architectural Design

Immanuel Kant (1724-1804)

Part II Cover

Immanuel Kant (1724-1804)

Is a German philosopher, who is a central figure in modern philosophy. Kant argued that the human mind creates the structure of human experience, that reason is the source of morality.

Part II	**Case Studies:** *Architectural Design*
Chapter 5	Sydney Opera House: *Risk vs. Innovation*
Chapter 6	Sydney Opera House: *Decision Making and Ethics*
Chapter 7	Fallingwater is Falling: *Creativity*
Chapter 8	Crystal Palace: *Design Expertise*
Chapter 9	Pruitt-Igoe: *A Nation's Conscience*

Ethical Decision Making in Architecture ● ÖMER AKIN

Utzon's initial sketches for Sydney Opera House, circa 1956

Chapter 5 Sydney Opera House: Risk: vs. Innovation

Introduction

One of the best known modern buildings of the 20th Century is the Sydney Opera House. For more than a half-century from its inception, it's celebrated as one of the most remarkable architectural edifices of the world. For over a decade, during the 50s and the 60s, it has been one of the largest and most visible construction projects anywhere in the world consuming significant attention of the Australian nation and that of the world's architectural intelligentsia.

The design created by the Danish architect, Jorn Utzon, has had no equal in terms of precedents or, for that matter, successors. Its construction was possible only because of an unprecedented political and professional resolve that overcame enormous technical, political, aesthetic, financial, and cultural obstacles. For our purposes the Sydney Opera House provides perhaps the most perfect case for studying Ethical Decision Making in Architecture.

Sydney Opera House illustrates, both intellectually and logistically, the full complexity of building delivery. It has tested the skills of practitioners to their limits, whether they are architects or engineers. Sophisticated Decision Making tools and strategies have been essential in its execution. Risk-Cost-Benefit Analysis method (Chapter 12) and Optimization (Chapter 14) were critical in making many of the key decisions. Planning (Chapter 13), a universal Decision Making method, was also used in the Sydney Opera House's delivery process.

These methods complement each other since the latter is primarily a synthetic approach while the former are analytic. The Sydney Opera House case also illustrates fundamental issues in ethics including the divergence between individual and institutional ethics, ethos,[xlv] and ethical plurality. For the designer, serving the greater good while serving the client is, to say the least, a difficult balancing act.

In this chapter we will address questions like "can the excesses of politicians and exuberance the designers, who bring about a masterpiece like the opera house, be excused for overextending public resources and compromising the buildings functionality? Does the designers' ethics begin and end with a commitment to design excellence? What about a commitment to the client or the users of their creation?

A Brief History[xlvi]

During the post-war years, the Sydney Opera House project became the symbol of Australian desire to create a world class cultural institution for the performing arts and in the process elevate the artistic consciousness of the entire nation. This idea predates the post-war years and can be observed in the actions of the first General Manager of the Australian Broadcasting Company, Mr. Charles Moses, and the first world renowned conductor of the Sydney Symphony Orchestra, Eugene Goossens, appointed to his post in 1946. There was no doubt that all major branches of the performing arts in Australia – opera, ballet, symphony, and subsequently theater – desperately needed a shot the arm.

Events, even at their highest levels, were being held in makeshift, retrofitted buildings with substandard staging facilities and small audience halls. The principal motivation for a new building grew from a clear sense of the inadequacy of existing facilities, which included poor audience capacity and inadequate backstage amenities. Throughout the evolution of this remarkable design and spectacular building, these factors were significant decision drivers.

In addition, while the competition documents for the Sydney Opera House included information about the site upon which it was to be placed, Bennelong Point at the Sydney Harbor; the local climate; and the prize money – 1st prize: £5,000; 2nd: £2,000; and 3rd: £1,000. Surprisingly, but perhaps not inconsistent with the ultimate goal of the project, no budget information was given. Was this an oversight? Did the government feel that the best design had to be obtained at any cost? Or did they assume that the cost of any reasonable design worthy of selection would not exceed a reasonable amount?

We will never know the answer to these questions with certainty. We can only be sure that, no promises were made to the potential winners regarding the implementation of their designs, which incidentally was explicitly stated in the competition documents. Also, even though the site of the project was located right along Sydney Harbor, no soil tests were conducted prior to the issuance of the competition. Anyone reasonably knowledgeable about buildings should have expected unfavorable foundation conditions at such a location. It is not clear from the records, but this also may have been an intentional omission. The organizers may have expected the competitors to take appropriate measures even without soil tests.

The Design

After the announcement of the international competition, 721 requests were made to obtain the competition documents. Seventy-nine of the potential competitors asked 470 questions about the terms of the competition. Entries came from 27 countries including Australia, Czechoslovakia, Denmark, UK, South Africa, US, French Morocco, Israel and Cyprus. On December 1956, 270 submissions were at hand to be reviewed by the four-man international panel of architects: Leslie Martin, Cobden Parkes, Eero Saarinen, and Harry Ashworth.

Saarinen, a key jury member arrived two days late, on January 11, 1957, and joined the jury review proceedings already in progress. After reviewing the projects discarded by the technical review panel as well as the fellow members of the jury, Saarinen came across the project submitted by Jorn Utzon. This project was eliminated on the grounds that it violated competition requirements by exceeding the site limits, particularly along its West border; and included elevations they were merely photographic enlargements that were imprecise depictions of the building's design (see this chapter's frontispiece).

Saarinen made an impassioned plea to the rest of the jury and had Utzon's project readmitted into the short list of projects being considered. Despite the open skepticism evident in the queries posed by his fellow jurors, Saarinen continued to point out the merits of this scheme. Facing criticism that questioned the feasibility of Utzon's design, he was willing to offer his own drawings to justify Utzon's submission.

Having just completed a shell structure of his own on the MIT campus, Saarinen was enthusiastic about the prospect of such a large scale implementation of shell structures. In the end, Utzon's project was given first prize. It was explained later that Saarinen was moved by the vision of this scheme due to its sensitivity towards the site and the harbor area within which it is located (Figure 6).

Realizing the Project

It was clear that this project had to be further detailed before it would be constructible. There was concern, even by one of the jurors, that the construction of the shell structure as proposed was not feasible. Early estimates indicated that the project would cost £4,800,000 and take up to five years to complete. This was clearly a lofty goal for the client and one, given the schedule and the non-existent budget, quite challenging.

In fact, during the 1958 elections, the key issue for the electorate was the state of the opera house competition. Premier Cahill was reelected with a small margin, running on the platform that he would continue to work towards building the opera house. His election victory meant that the project would continue. During the next few years, the construction documents of the project were begun as state-run lotteries were used to raise the required funds.

One of the other fortunate developments was the commissioning of Ove Arup and Associates as project engineers. Their experience with shell structures and large projects turned out to be a key for the eventual success of the design.

Figure 6 Sydney Opera House at Sydney Harbor

Figure 7 The composition of the Opera House's design: the lower podium and upper shell structures

Primarily due to Arup Associates' input, the project was divided into two stages: the lower podium and the upper shell structure (Figures 7 and 8). The partitioning of the building into two major stages was more than a logical one. It served to organize the construction process and gain time for the design of the shell structure. It was also part of Utzon's original conception of the scheme. He stated that his inspiration came from the Mayan temples of the Yucatan, in Mexico. when he wrote:

The platform as an architectural element is a fascinating feature. I first fell in love with it in Mexico on a study trip in 1949 where I found many variations. A great strength radiates from them. By introducing the platform with a level at the same height as the jungle top, these people had suddenly obtained a new dimension in life. On these high situated platforms – many of them as high as 100 meters – they built their temples.

Utzon did not intend to build a temple, at least not literally, but this metaphor served him well in providing a massive and stable foundation from which his dynamic sail like forms sprung. The visual and functional relationships between the podium and the roof forms were convincing and well-conceived. The podium contained all of the functional spaces, pedestrian access and movement spaces, the auditoria and smaller theater spaces. The podium upon which the sail like shells of the building were to be placed constituted the first stage of the construction. In addition, the sail-like roof forms supported by the podium enclosed the major assembly halls, and provided striking visual and acoustic expression, which are two of the significant functions of the upper structure.

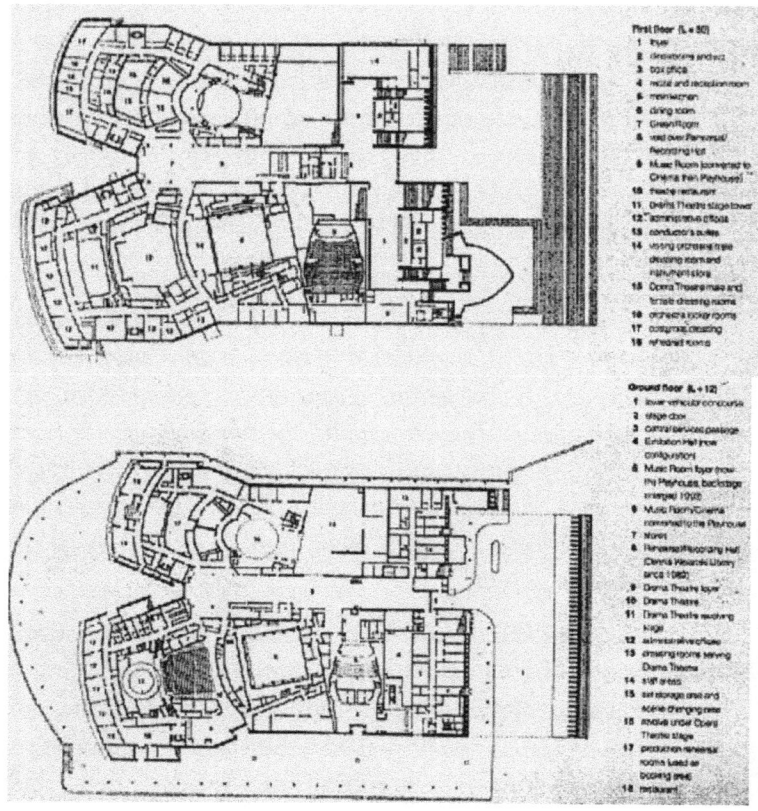

Figure 8 Ground and 1st Floor Plans of Sydney Opera House's podium levels

Subsequently, under Arup's guidance, Utzon was persuaded to radically revise the geometry of the shell structure (Figure 9), thus making its construction feasible (Figure 10). Later new stages were also added, such as interior finishes, furnishings and roof tiles (Figure 11).

As Utzon and Arup were busy refining the final geometry of the proposed design, so that the size and makeup of structural components could be accurately estimated, the client was still refining his requirements for the building. In June of 1958, the committee of Sydney Opera House made changes to the administration area, workshops, and dining rooms. On July 2, 1958, it was announced that the building would now contain an experimental theater with 400 seats. Two days later, a television broadcasting studio was added to the wish list. In September of the same year, the orchestra pit was enlarged to 120 musicians instead of 105.

Construction of the Podium

Construction officially began in August 1958 after the demolition of the existing structure at Bennelong Point. Except for being the burial spot of Mr. Bennelong, arguably the best known aboriginal liaison captured by the early settlers in Australia, this location had housed indistinct facilities up to 1958.

The contractor for Stage I, Civil and Civic was the lowest bidder with £1,397,929, 40% less than the highest bidder. It was speculated that this was a deliberate move to gain this high profile contract and make up the difference through change orders. This was a well-placed wager by Civil and Civic. The estimated completion time of 18 months was more than doubled by the time Stage I was substantially complete. The reasons for the delay included incomplete construction documents, unexpected foundation conditions, and design revisions of the podium and the upper structure.[xlvii]

Figure 9 Utzon's model for the derivation spherical forms for Sydney Opera House's structure

In March 1961, with the podium only three quarters complete, contractors Civil and Civic complained in writing that the "*contract has been a long history of changes, frustrations, inability to logically plan the work due to the lack of information and detail..*" After 21 months into the job, out of a total of 700 drawings and 695 amendments only 55% were completed. Of the 1,500 items in the original provisional bill of quantities 500 were never used while 500 new ones were generated.[xlviii]

One of the critical areas of design, redesign, testing, and deployment was the concourse area which was spanned by 50 pre-stressed folded beams 6' wide and up to 4' 6" deep, with some spans exceeding 160'. The midpoint supports for these beams shown in the original design were eliminated and folded beam cross-sections were revised into a T-shape, at one end, that gradually transformed into a rectangular shape, at the other end.

In addition, the foundations consisted of 460 piers of various depths (20'-70') depending on non-uniform soil conditions. Due to the lack of early soil tests, some of this was discovered only during the construction stage. Also, the design called for "occupiable" spaces below the water table. The orchestra pit, for example, was 15' below. This contributed to escalating construction costs by leading to extensive excavation during construction, and subsequent waterproofing.

There were several important reasons for the litany of design changes. First, Utzon had very high design standards. When faced with the bitter consequence of falling behind schedule and budget, he held the belief that "design never ends," striving continuously to perfect his design.

Figure 10 In-situ erection of the ribbed shell structure of the Sydney Opera House

Complicating matters were several alternative construction technologies being considered by Arup Associates: such as, thin shell, ribbed shell, and steel frame. Early in 1961, the prevailing opinion on the part of almost all involved began to shift to a ribbed structure accompanied by a spherical geometry (Figure 10).

Eventually, Utzon himself was also convinced and modified the shape of the ribbed-shell structure into a spherical geometry. He provided the exact change of the new "shell" design with his now famous model using sliced-off segments from a wooden sphere to create the curves of the entire shell language of the Sydney Opera House (Figure 9). This was a watershed moment for the design. It made the structural design of the roof forms possible while causing a great deal of public speculation and private consternation.

Having gained valuable experience in Stage I, the selection of the contractor for Stage II was done differently. Hornibooks Inc. was invited to carry out Stage II. They not only had construction expertise but were also nearly as sophisticated in engineering design as was Arup Associates. During the course of the shell structure's design, Hornibooks developed several novel computer applications. They were by and large responsible for the successful completion of this stage of the project, even though the project went through, even more drastic, political, technical, and financial challenges.

The added dead loads due to the shift to a ribbed concrete shell meant that the support columns –70' long with bases 7'-15' in diameter, with 28' below ground and 42' above ground – had to be redesigned, demolished and recast, adding to the ballooning project budget.

Figure 11 Roof tile modules and assembly of the ribbed shell structure

The ribbed-shell roof had to be broken down into similarly shaped pre-stressed segments to facilitate prefabrication. Since the curvature was spherical this became possible. In fact, the possibility of prefabrication was one of the principal motivations for the shift to the spherical form. The shell modules had to be designed to hold temporary pre-stressing during the construction stage since with the curvilinear form of the roof scaffolding was virtually impossible. To create lateral bracing between the ribbed modules, sophisticated bolting and sealing details had to be developed (Figure 10).

The roof tiles were also designed in modular form in order to enable factory production (Figure 11). This complicated the ribbed shell design even further.

Sydney and its Seminal Building

In spite of these practical problems, the design and its architect achieved instant and worldwide notoriety. Never before witnessed in the annals of architectural history, many hailed the project as visionary while others ridiculed its unusual appearance.

However, lack of funding was the most often used justification to try to abandon the project. In 1966, as political pressures mounted and a newly elected government that ran on a platform against the project came to power, the project fell into difficult times. When another firm was appointed to take over interior design, Utzon complained that his design authority was being undermined. Further, payment of fees was being delayed by the new government.

In a drastic move, Utzon resigned his position in February of 1966 prior to the completion of Stage II and commencement of the building's interior construction. This led to further schedule delays and cost overruns. Australian firm Hall, Todd and Livermore supervised the remaining stages of construction and interior design. The project was completed in nearly 12 years after its inception and after realizing expenditures of £60 million, more than a 1000% increase over initial estimates.

Today, the building stands as the pride-inspiring symbol of Sydney, and indeed of entire Australia, far surpassing the impact originally expected. Today, it has a full schedule of artistic performances. There are however some wrinkles, which, after 50 years of existence, have not been completely ironed out.

The main hall is the exclusive territory of the Sydney Symphony. This moved the opera and ballet functions to the smaller, secondary halls. In addition the theater function was moved out of the upper halls into rooms of the podium space. Three smaller halls with smaller seating capacities of 350, 389, and 530 seats were converted into theater functions This game of musical chairs that started during the construction of the building still continues to this day.

All of this has led to three, major programmatic complications. Owing to the unique forms used in the design of the building, the seating capacity in the two main halls, symphony and opera, are limited to 2,679 and 1,547 seats, respectively. This underrepresents their desired capacities. Also, due to the limitations imposed by the shell form, the size of the backstage area is restricted. Additions and modifications are nearly impossible since enclosure of the podium levels had to be high-stress concrete in order to resists moisture penetration and structural forces ever present in the harbor basin.

In order to fully realize performance functions, some of the other functions of the building were converted. Space in office and storage areas has been curtailed; lobby areas have been minimized; and areas for circulation are occasionally used to store portable furniture. The library function has been disbanded to make room for one of the most recent theater facilities, thereby donating the Sydney Opera House library collection to other local libraries.

At the beginning of the entire effort, Sydney Opera House was justified on the basis that existing facilities did not serve Australia's performing arts needs well enough. These facilities were considered deficient in: audience capacity, back stage inflexibility, and lack of up-to-date amenities.

After 12 years and £60,000,000, Sydney became the proud owner of a world-renowned architectural symbol but, ironically, its national halls of symphony, ballet and opera still possess facilities that leave some aspects of functionality wanting; perhaps a predicament not unusual for an edifice more than half a century old and serving many more masters than any ordinary building would.

Before the completion of the building, Jorn Utzon, the architect who gave Sydney it's architectural and civic identity left Australia prematurely, never to return. To add insult to injury, according to Jon's architect son Jan Utzon, because of his resignation, Jorn was sanctioned by the Danish Society of Architects, and was banned from receiving government commissions.

Some of the most significant ethical considerations in this case are illustrated by Jan Utzon's recollections of the events of four decades ago, at which time he was a student of architecture in Sydney. Currently, the administration of the Sydney Opera House has decided to rehire Utzon's office, under Jan's directive, to reconfigure the building in order to recreate the original design intent.

ETHICAL DECISION MAKING IN ARCHITECTURE ● ÖMER AKIN

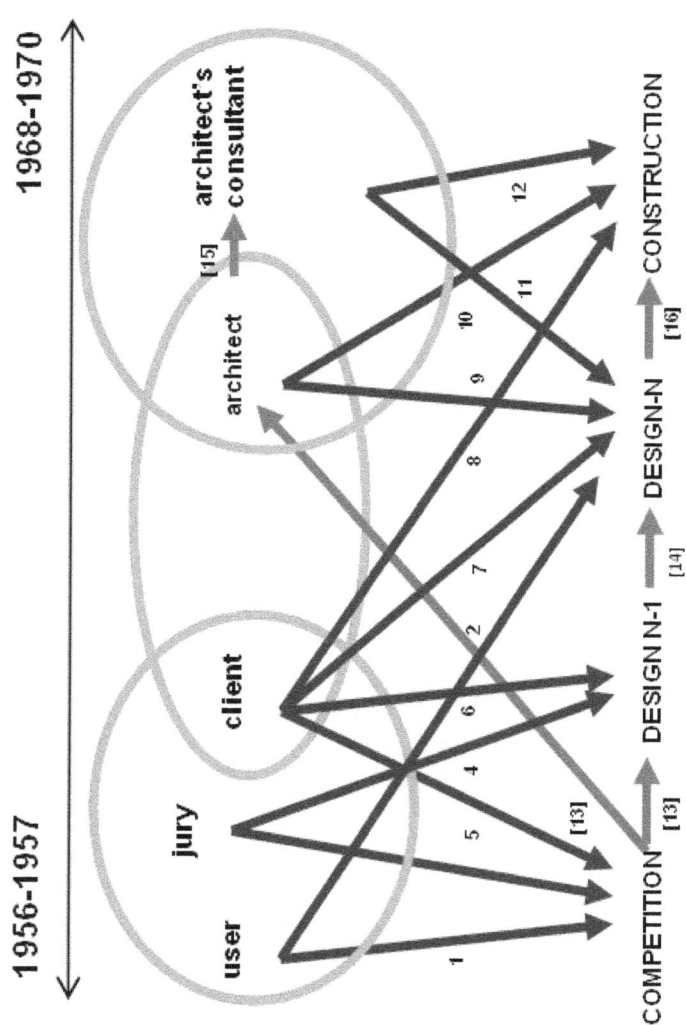

Figure 12 Workflow diagram of the Sydney Opera House

Chapter 6 Sydney Opera House: Decision Making and Ethics

Good planners develop ideas about how they should proceed through the design delivery process. They define goals, sub-goals, and recursively breakdown their tasks into discrete acts that can be carried out with non-overwhelming cognitive loads and no likelihood of backtracking.

In the case of the workflow of Sydney Opera House we see such behavior in action, involving many agents, undertaking multiple tasks, using diverse knowledge domains, often over a multi-year schedule (Figure 12).

o The clients of Sydney Opera House, including Premiere Cahill, conductor Goossens, and other public officials created an international competition to obtain the best ideas possible for the design and construction of the opera house (Figure 12, #5).
o This process resulted in the assembly of the competition jury, consisting of Leslie Martin, Cobden Parkes, Eero Saarinen, and Harry Ashworth (Figure 12, #3).
o It also ended up creating a complex users group consisting of politicians, tax payers, news media, and other interested parties (Figure 12, #1).
o This became an important voice, if not a direct decision agent, in the delivery process. Once the competition solicitation was published, submissions were received (Figure 12, #4); and a selection was made (Figure 12, #6).
o The architect, the principal player for the rest of the project's lifecycle, was identified (Figure 12, #13).

o In turn the architect selected the consulting engineers (Figure 12, #14).
o As these events unraveled through successive design refinements, the project progressed towards the building's ultimate construction and occupancy (Figure 12, #2, #7, #8, #9, #10., #11, #12).

The entire process took a dozen years, thousands of man-hours of work by a myriad of specialists resulting in a volume of documentation that is impossible to briefly summarize. This case has the unmistakable markings of an ill-defined problem (Chapter 10). The program brief which is the official document defining the requirement specifications has major information gaps, including, no soil tests, no budget, no commitment to build the selected project and many changes in design requirements.

In retrospect, it is clear that the lack of soil testing contributed to the project's excessive delays and cost overruns. Lack of a budget excused some of the cost increases but in the end became one of the factors that spoiled the relationship between the client and the architect. Additionally, this affected the way in which the construction was completed. It is fair speculation that, if he was in charge of the end phase of the project, his interior design would have resulted in a more successful and economical outcome.

The volatility in the project delivery stage occurred due to the repeated modifications of the architectural program. These include late additions to the design requirements: such as, the administrative wing, workshop space, dining area, an experimental theater, the TV broadcasting studio and the enlargement of the orchestra pit.

Furthermore, the implicit, if not explicit, demotion of critical items, such as the total number of seats required, the fractured theatre space, and the inadequate backstage facilities contributed to volatility in the planning process.

The design process is notoriously unruly. It is not unusual that a program can be changed as a function of the particular design selected by the competition jury, especially when the criteria for design are either not explicitly stated or altered as the process goes on. These are tell-tale signs of an ill-defined problem (Chapter 10). In this project context, the volatility of the design problem was not limited to just these issues. The elliptical form of the shell structure did not lend itself to accurate calculation. The shell elements' center of gravity did not lie within their base, making them unstable with a tendency to topple over. To make this project feasible meant changing the entire geometry of the shells, going to a heavier construction system and as a result demolishing and recasting the building's foundations.

How do designers manage such volatility? Planning a goal hierarchy through which the given problem is decomposed into discrete and well-defined parts is a principal strategy (Chapter 10). In this case, we see evidence of this in the separation of the project into two phases. Incidentally this phasing strategy corresponds almost exactly to Utzon's original design concept.

In the first, podium stage, the functional components of the building complex were constructed using poured-in-place concrete technology, while in the second, shell-structure stage, the performance volumes and outside appearance of the building was completed using pre-fabrication technology. The ribbed-shell structure required innovative design and construction methods. Its assembly without formwork required the erection of curved forms, necessitating post-tensioned assembly (Figure 10).

Consequently, deep pylons were required to be poured into the harbor sub-strata, upsetting the careful allocation of the precious square footage of the building that was allocated to program functions. In the end, the delivery of the Sydney Opera House can be seen as the culmination of thousands of individual decisions.

Can we consider this complex Decision Making case a successfully planned and executed one? If so how can we account for the more than tenfold cost increase and nearly threefold delay in delivery time? How can we justify the programmatic shortcomings of the final product?

Risk-Cost-Benefit Analysis

The most obvious decisions of risk taken in the case of the Sydney Opera House include:
- selection of Utzon's design
- commissioning of Utzon with the working drawings
- selection of Civil & Civic, the first phase contractors
- commissioning Ove Arup as the structural engineer
- changing the elliptical geometry into a spherical one
- pushing out Utzon from the project

Let us now examine each of these from a Decision Making standpoint. To do this, first we have to examine the basics of Risk-Cost-Benefit (RCB) analysis, which is a specific decision tool that takes into account potential gains and losses of each action (Chapter 11). If these factors are known with a high degree of certainty, there is little or no risk involved. Choices can be safely based on the total sum of the gains and losses. When there is high uncertainty, as was the case in this case, risks are involved and the estimation of potential gains and losses makes RCB a difficult proposition.

Selection of Utzon's Design

For the Sydney Opera House, the selection of Utzon's design was the beginning of risk taking. The jury converged on a design for which there was serious concern about its structural feasibility. Only through Saarinen's personal assurances that this concern could be alleviated just long enough to make the selection. The cost of this risk included abandonment of the project, delays, cost overruns, poor building functionality, and collateral damage to political figures involved in the building delivery process. All but the first of these cost factors became a reality. In fact, the project was saved only through many sacrifices. The jury, wittingly or unwittingly pitted its own risk taking against those of the clients'.

The benefit that outweighed these drawbacks, almost singularly, has been the notoriety Sydney Opera House brought to Sydney, Australia. How could such a risk be divined by the jury so prophetically? This is where the jury's credentials, the Australian government's backing, public proclamations to the architectural intelligentsia, even the media frenzy about the shortcomings of the initial design fueled the fires of Sydney Opera House's climb to stardom.

In Toker's words, once the "spin" is on, the "buzz" about the building will keep it in the architectural orbit for many a decade to come, making it the darling of tourists and architectural connoisseurs. This then turned out to be the benefit that justified all sins. The *Theory of Design Added Value* in fact shows how such contradictory outcomes can be justified and explained by Architectural Decision Making techniques (Chapter 10).[xlix]

Was this "good" Decision Making? Only if we see the interests of the jury and the client as independent factors or have a sure-bet for the notoriety of the design. Through the boldness of the jury's sense of self-confidence this decision became a self-fulfilling prophecy. Otherwise, we would have to claim serendipity as the only explanation which is unacceptable as a credible Decision Making strategy.

Commissioning Utzon to do the working drawings

Once selected, the design was in the hands of Jorn Utzon, a young architect without the high level of experience that would be a requisite for realizing the production drawings of such a challenging project. Did the client make the right decision to leave things entirely in Utzon's hands and in fact requiring fast tracking, one of the most difficult delivery processes in the field of building construction? The risks taken in the budgeting process was enormous. Consequently, design retrofits, construction challenges, incomplete detailing, and the delivery schedule spiraling out of control could have been expected.

What was the benefit that was expected through this decision? Keeping Utzon's signature that of a hitherto unknown name in the annals of architecture at the time, unexpectedly gave a boost to its notoriety factor. Thus once the design was selected, despite long odds, a self-confident Utzon went along with that decision making and everyone realized the benefits.

Commissioning Arup with the structural design

Arup's reputation and track record made his firm suitable for the job. In such a challenging task, appropriate experience and sophisticated design technology is the minimum that would be necessary. True to this assessment, Arup's design team was right for the task. After chalking up three years of design work to mere experience, and losing some of their best designers; Arup started from scratch and realized the project in the only way it could have been realized by changing the geometry of the shell-structure.

Arup's firm worked with Utzon's decisions all along and created a building that is structurally sound and technically sophisticated. For the construction technology of the day, its erection without the aid of formwork is almost miraculous. Its stability upon the weak soil of Sydney Harbor is another great achievement.

Selection of Civil and Civic as first contractors

In contrast to the selection of Ove Arup, Civil and Civics' selection as the contractors of Phase I defies the set of criteria emphasized by the RCB model. The risk of hiring an underbidding contractor was deemed less significant than that of cost savings. In the end, this backfired as the cost overruns all but eliminated any savings to be realized and introduced additional costs and delays.

Changing the geometry of the shell structure

This decision was a must. Without it the design would not have been realized and all would be lost. This decision delayed the inevitable, and cost dearly in terms of time and money. Utzon's persistence kept everyone focused on a shared goal. Soon he too realized that this goal was being pursued at the expense of all else that mattered. In the end, Utzon decided to alter the geometry of the design, relieving the anxiety built-up at several circles close to the project.

It is hard to believe that the hype created by a challenged design could be a calculated decision strategy. Accidental, yes; but not calculated. Hence, we have to chalk another one to serendipity. The timing in switching to the circular geometry should have occurred earlier. However, in a world of sound Decision Making it qualifies as nothing short of brilliant, despite its belated arrival.

Alienating Utzon and causing his resignation

In the end, the new client representative ushered in by the electorate forced Utzon out. Once the project was on its way to becoming a reality, there was worldwide recognition of its exceptional visual and spatial qualities. With each obstacle being overcome, be it resetting of the foundations, erection of the ribbed shells, or the cladding of the tiles, the reputation of the building grew. Utzon had already served his useful purpose and became dispensable so far as the ultimate goal of Sydney Opera House was concerned.

Ethical Considerations

In the Sydney Opera House, there are a plethora of issues that we can discuss under the topic of ethics. Let us frame this discussion with the help of three central issues:

o   Divergence of institutional and individual ethics,
o   Divergence of architectonics vs. ethics, and
o   Multiplicity of ethical frameworks.

Divergence of Institutional and Individual Ethics

When Utzon submitted his design, he perhaps unwittingly pitched his artistic prowess against his professional integrity. Artistically, he was reaching for the "best" design he could conceive. Almost in an Aristotelian zeal he was proposing the best that anyone, not just he, could offer. Simultaneously and implicitly, he was also saying: "take my professional word that this is qualified to meet your (the client's) design requirement." Not only such a product would have to be presented in a way that convinces others of its feasibility but that it would indeed have to be feasible.

Utzon, in meeting his personal commitment to design excellence, pitted his professional standard: to uphold the most obvious obligation an architect has towards a client; against advancing his personal standards of excellence. However rational this line of questioning may be, it is particularly cruel to Utzon. How can we find a building, which is arguably the most acclaimed architectural product of the Australian continent, in breach of ethics due to professional shortcomings?

The fallacy of this statement is in the virtue labeled "cruel," or inversely "kind." With this, we fall into the ethical framework of the individual's Virtue Ethics rather than confronting the moral obligation of professional service that is to meet the needs of the client. Utzon is not alone in recognizing that this built-in conflict between the professional self vs. the professional institution. Cuff gives voice to an anonymous architect articulating just such a conflict that she faced almost on a daily basis (Chapter 4, page 29).

While the relative importance of the purposes vying for the architect's professional conscience varies from case to case, successful practitioners know how to establish workable priorities between the goals of the individual, the office and the profession, just as the anonymous architect tries to do. In order to maintain a consistent ethical stance, the architect must be cognizant of the need to establish orders of priority between the multiple levels of responsibility. Without such priorities they are likely to overlook important moral issues.

Before Utzon decided to change the elliptical design into a spherical one, in order to render it structurally feasible, his project calendar had already exceeded the allowed time and the available budget. And in the end, Sydney Opera House turned out to be a building with a spectacular image and functionality. Utzon's dilemma was exasperated by the need to successfully meet client's ever changing requirements. Assuming that this is an idiosyncrasy of the architectural field, is it also a sufficient condition to ensure adequate morality standards? This is the most difficult question architects have to wrestle with.

Architects, however competent they may be, are also morally accountable for the social outcomes of their designs. The matter of the correctness of their products, as distinct from aesthetic aspects, is the purview of ethos[1] not ethics. An unskilled surgeon who inadvertently harms a client is morally superior to one who is skilled but who deliberately maims his/her patients. Yet this distinction is likely to escape well-meaning professional moralists. They mistakenly equate professional ethics with professional ethos, expressed through personal integrity and design excellence.

Divergence of architectonics vs. ethics

The architect is responsible for imparting distinctive esthetical qualities to buildings they design. The proper fulfillment of the architect's responsibilities requires competent and impartial service, not only on behalf of the client, but also in the interest of the public. Seldom does a building affect only its owner, nor does it stand alone. For this reason, the architect is responsible for designing buildings that protect health, safety and welfare of all who use them and enhance the environment by shouldering due regard to existing physical factors, and use patterns.

Multiplicity of ethical frameworks

If we were magically transported to the moment when Utzon submitted his design proposal to the Sydney Opera House competition, how would we advise him? Alternatively, if we were in the same position as Saarinen, would we advocate Utzon's scheme? Let's consider these questions one at a time.

The Sydney Opera House has been everything the initiators of the building hoped it would be. Charles Moses, the director of the symphony, Eugene Goossens, its first world renowned conductor, and Joseph Cahill, the Premier of New South Wales, were all looking to create an institution that would place Australia's performing arts on the world map. They also realized that this would take not only the assembly of a world class group of artists, musicians and performers but also the creation of a world class venue. Beyond everyone's wildest dreams, the building, almost single-handedly achieved this, and more.

It made Sydney a destination for an ever increasing number of tourists and the Opera House a must-see among the world's most coveted architectural landmarks. In the final analysis, the building's performance aspect is the unexpected underachiever. Its facilities are limited in terms of the backstage, lobby space, theatre spaces, number of seats in the main halls, storage spaces, and auxiliary functions. Would we then wish that Utzon had never submitted his scheme or better yet started on it earlier so that he had enough time to make his brilliant design feasible and functional?

In advising Utzon we may find our advice to be potentially infringing on the rights of all of the other competitors who submitted "feasible" and "complete" documents. (Here, Saarinen is also culpable, but that comes later.) Also we would be infringing on the public's right to be prudent, or at least not wasteful with funds; the artist's right to perform in a functionally superior facility; and the contractor's right to work from a consistent and complete set of drawings and specifications.

In advising him not to submit we would find ourselves squarely against many ardent admirers of the building. This includes the world tourist, the tourism sector of Australia, the architectural community, the engineering and construction sector, and the media which incessantly uses the building as a backdrop for their public messaging. With a negative recommendation, would we not have infringed on their rights?

Saarinen's circumstance is also fraught with similar conflicts. Picking a scheme from the technical-reject pile and advocating it until it wins is infringement on the rights of all other competitors. The next level of infringement occurs when we find Saarinen actually offering his own ideas about how the scheme could be realized. Here he crosses over the line between an impartial judge of quality to being a co-author of a submitted scheme. This violates the rights of all who favor a fair jury process.

A position of passivity for Saarinen should elicit the same kind of objection we already articulated in Utzon's case: risking the loss of an opportunity! Who would want to pass up on an architectural masterpiece on account of mere technicalities or officious nay-sayers? Innovation and creativity are not for the faint hearted! Innovation takes courage and facing risks. A jury's duty includes finding the most creative submission. And that, my friends, takes the kind of courage displayed by Saarinen, who did not hesitate to bend a few rules in order to give the world Utzon's brilliant design.

Both advocacies presented on behalf of these individuals illustrate the tenet of pluralistic adjudication where rival frameworks support conflicting choices. Deontological (rights-based) ethics would compel us to protect the rights of other competitors and reject Utzon's scheme. Teleological (consequence-based) ethics would have us accept the scheme by outweighing the functional shortcoming of the building in favor of its aesthetic accolades. Finally, Aristotelian (virtue-based) ethics would suggest that Saarinen should have refrained from promoting the shell structure of the scheme, just because he himself had one built in Boston. Self-promotion or worse yet vanity would have been the infraction in that case.

Any self-respecting applied ethicist knows that there are just too many ethical frameworks that apply to any given case at hand. More often than not these frameworks point to divergent results, particularly for the cases of professional ethicists, who know that adjudication is not a clear cut process.

Therefore the ethicist-architect, or just an everyday ethical architect, must realize that the world of ethics is multi-pronged. A pluralist view is inevitable and a negotiated adjudication is unavoidable. In the world of applied ethics, gone are the days of the ivory-tower ethicist who can dissect the case so finely that a singular truth emerges.

In today's world of applied ethics, all parties must be cognizant of rival ethical frameworks and be prepared to negotiate towards a mutually acceptable solution that has a pluralistic stance, not only in terms of multiple constituents but also in terms of multiple ethical frameworks that must be satisfied (Chapter 10). One who ignores the rival ethical frameworks or the potentially conflicting interests of other constituents does so at one's own peril.

ETHICAL DECISION MAKING IN ARCHITECTURE ● ÖMER AKIN

Scenic view of Fallingwater, Bear Run, Pennsylvania

Chapter 7 Fallingwater is Falling: Creativity

Background

The design process has been under careful study since the late 60's. To date there are several hundred studies conducted with designers, documenting not only what they design but *how* they design. The fields that have been engaged in this kind of research include architecture, industrial design, mechanical engineering, electrical and computer engineering, chemical engineering, and civil engineering. In each of these fields there is either a major- or a sub-area that involves the design of a class of objects: such as, buildings, appliances, machines, electronic circuitry, chemical plants, and large structures.

The examination of the process in each area reveals a variety of methodological approaches. Some involve interviews and document reviews after the design is complete. These are called Retrospective Reviews. Others involve recording of the process as it happens for subsequent analyses. This is called Protocol Analysis.[li] Yet others consider the design in its historical context to discern the designer's intentions. This is what we know as Historical Analysis, as practiced by architectural historians. As an example of Retrospective Reviews, we know that Edgar J. Kaufmann told Mr. Wright:

"My money has bought me great many fine things in life, but none of them have brought me greater joy than the house you built for me on Bear Run."

Of course, he was speaking, of Fallingwater, a structure so remarkable, so romantic, so perfectly in harmony with its setting that it is understandably the most famous private residence in the world.[lii]

Edgar Kaufmann, Jr. Joined the Taliesin Fellowship in 1934, and shortly after urged his father to support and fund the building as an example of Mr. Wright's alternative proposal to urban centralization called the *Broadacre City*. Mr. Kaufmann gave his full endorsement to this proposal.

During one of Wright's trips to Pittsburgh the Kaufmanns took him out to the site near Bear Run where they owned a weekend cottage situated in a forest glen abundant with rhododendron bushes and waterfalls. The site so appealed to Mr. Wright's creative genius that he wrote of his first glimpse of it in December, 1934:

"the visit to the waterfall in the woods stays with me and a domicile has taken vague shape in my mind to the music of the stream. When contours come you will see it."[liii]

In fact the design was to be one of the most innovative conceptions of residential architecture where the building's natural context became a remarkable form giver and the basis of the designer's expression of a completely new set of principles. In a TV film on Fallingwater produced by Kent State University[liv] Edgar Kaufmann, Jr. recalls their first trip to Bear Run:

"When my parents invited Wright to visit the property with the idea that he might design a house for them, they took him around the property and explained why the existing house was influenced and no longer very happily located. They also took him down to the waterfalls and explained that they

spent basking on the flat rock at the base of the falls, walking in under the falls, getting a massage, sliding down into the potholes, and having fun. And the falls, including the drama of the water's movement and the charm of the noise that it made, were something that everybody appreciated a great deal. This was a focus for us. Wright took that in, he didn't make any comment, but he once said that since we wanted to move farther away from the highway than the old house, that somewhere nearer the falls might be quite agreeable."

Edgar Kaufmann Jr. also comments:

"Eventually when he designed the first scheme for the house, which was also the last scheme, he placed it as we all know directly above the waterfall, which I do not think had ever crossed my parent's minds (Figure 13). *But once having been presented with the notion they had no resistance to it at all, it seemed perfectly good and proper."*[lv]

Proper may not be exactly the correct description, at least in hindsight, as this placement has been the catalyst for Wright's extraordinary creation more than any other factor, as well as leading to complications and difficulties the building went through, during its stages of design, construction and occupancy.

The contractor of the house was a local builder who, while competent in conventional methods, clearly had not done anything like this before. As a result, some of the early stonework had to be redone, but more seriously the reinforcing work of the cantilevered floor slabs were questioned by the client and became a source of contention for the project.

Figure 13: Cross sections of Fallingwater, Pennsylvania

Figure 14: Livingroom of Fallingwater, Pennsylvania

The Kaufmanns spent their weekends in the house from 1939 on to the end of their lives. Since then Edgar, Jr. has given the house to the Western Pennsylvania Conservancy so that it might be cared for and kept open to the public.[lvi] Each year, thousands visit Fallingwater to enjoy its spectacular interior (Figure 14).

What these visitors do not know is that Fallingwater was victimized by several serious problems that became ongoing struggles for the owners and trustees of the property. One of these is the repeated breach of the moisture barriers of the building's roof surfaces; and another one is the sagging and cracking of the structural slabs. Wright was confident in his design and drew from earlier experiences, in particular the Imperial Hotel in Tokyo that possessed similar cantilevers.

The circumstances that led to disagreements between client and architect are illustrated in the correspondence between them during the building's construction phase. In order to gain a clearer understanding of how one can adjudicate the ethical issues that arise, let us do a retrospective review of what transpired by sampling some of the letters from Millar's exceptional documentation in *Frank Lloyd Wright Letters to Clients*.[lvii]

The Letters

Letter (1) May 4th 1936[lviii]
Mr. Edgar J. Kaufmann
Kaufmann Department Stores
Pittsburgh, Pennsylvania

Dear E.J.:

You seem the forget all I said about building an extraordinary house in extraordinary circumstances. Having been through it scores of times I know what we are up against and decline to start it unless I can see our way...

Now suppose I was a sculptor and you would say "carve me an extraordinary statue." I would accept. Then you would hand me a pantograph and say – "use this." I have found the use off the pantograph a good way to carve statues. It saves time and money. Then I would say – "but in this case it will waste both time and money and ruin the statue." You would come back with "but then I have statues made I have the pantograph used."

Well, E.J., you would have the sculptor where you have me now with your thumb. I can't build this extraordinary house with a thumb. Read the enclosed correspondence and note the pantograph punctilio for only one thing. There is no sense whatever of the things he [Carl F. Thumm, Kaufmann's assistant manager, who presented Mr. Kaufmann in matters pertaining to the building of the house] *should know after studying the plans.*

Now a pickaxe is more suited to my style of labor than a pantograph. But, for a fact, I can't use either. Your thumb won't do. I must have my own fingers. I want to make a success of this house if I have a chance.

A chance means very largely having my own way with my own work using my own fingers. Your thumb might be helpful in his place. His place wouldn't be trying to use me (fools rush where angels fear to tread) to get your house built by letting me use him.

This ought to clear up point one and get me a modest builder with brains – not too anxious to show off – willing to learn new ways of doing old things. Able but wise to the fact that his previous experience might fool him in this case. I know the type. I've worked with scores of them. Can't you send somebody here to me for a few days that I can initiate?

Again, if I were a sculptor you could say "all right bring your own tools." But being an architect hundreds of miles away and a house for you in question I have to find my tools near you. I have explained all this to you many times.

Now about money.

You seem suspicious when I ask for it, and use the scissors to clip the sum. Don't be afraid. You aren't going to pay much nor pay much too soon.

You won't be let down so don't you let me down.

Sincerely yours,
Frank Lloyd Wright

Letter (2) May 13, 1936[lix]

Mr. Walter Hall
Kaufmann Department Stores
Fort Alleghany, Pennsylvania

Dear Mr. Hall:

We have a house, chiefly masonry —stonework and concrete—which we are to build at Bear Run, Pennsylvania for Mr. Edgar J. Kaufmann of Kaufmann's Department Stores in Pittsburgh. We have learned about you through one of the young men in Taliesin Fellowship, Earl Friar, and conceived the idea that you might be of help in the construction of the house.

If this is of interest to you, you might care to meet us in Pittsburgh? On what basis would your services be available to us in this connection?

Sincerely Yours, Frank Lloyd Wright

Letter (3) May 31, 1936[lx]

Mr. Edgar J. Kaufmann
Kaufmann Department Stores
Pittsburgh, Pennsylvania

Dear E.J.:

We are on the way early this week. I am looking upon Hall as the contracting builder for your house – on some fair set price and percentage basis. He will accept and you will be pleased with [him]. *I do not furnish a supervisor on the job except as we arrange for one – between us.*

My object in getting Hall on the job is to save you that expense and insure cooperation with me. Probably some talk is necessary to clear up this point between us. But don't get headed in wrong on these matters.

See you soon –
Frank Lloyd Wright, Architect

Letter (4) July 13, 1936[lxi]
Mr. Edgar J. Kaufmann
Kaufmann Department Stores
Pittsburgh, Pennsylvania

My dear Edgar:

A note from Hall says he is on the job now and would have been ten days ago but for your Thumm in the soup again.

These officious yes-men make their boss more trouble in the end than they could ever pay for in cheese-pairings. Isn't that style of business distinctly dated? I thought so.

As always,
Frank Lloyd Wright

Letter (5) August 26, 1936[lxii]

Mr. Edgar J. Kaufmann
Kaufmann Department Stores
Pittsburgh, Pennsylvania
My dear E.J.:

If you are paying to have the concrete engineering done down there, there is no use whatever in our doing it here. I am willing you should take it over but I am not willing to be insulted.

So we will send no more steel diagrams. I am unaccustomed to such treatment where I have built buildings before and do not intend to put up with it now, so I am calling Bob [Bob Moser] back until we can work out something or nothing.

Also it appears that an attitude has developed on your part – "what does the architect know about what I want – I am going to live in this house – not he." Now I have heard that provincialism from women but never before from a man. And it isn't too late yet for you to get an architect that does know what you want.

I don't know what kind of architect you are familiar with but it apparently isn't the kind I think I am. You seem to know how to treat a decent one.

I have put so much more into this house than you or any other client has a right to expect that if I haven't your confidence – to hell with the whole thing.

Sincerely yours,
Frank Lloyd Wright

Telegram AUGUST 27TH[lxiii]
BOB MOSER:

DROP WORK AND COME BACK IMMEDIATELY WE ARE THROUGH UNTIL KAUFMANN AND I ARRIVE AT SOME BASIS OF MUTUAL RESPECT. YOU ARE NEEDED HERE. DO NOT DELAY ONE HOUR AND BRING ALL PLANS YOU CAN GET. IF YOU HAVE NO MONEY DRAW ON ME FARMERS STATE BANK.

FRANK LLOYD WRIGHT

Letter (6) August 29, 1936[lxiv]
Mr. Walter J. Hall
Kaufmann's Bear Run Camp
Pittsburgh, Pennsylvania

My dear Hall:

I guess I took too much for granted when I called you on the Kaufmann house. Probably you have always been your own boss, never worked for an architect and never had ethics.

At any rate it appears from Bob's letters that you are undertaking to advise Kaufmann concerning various matters that are certainly my business and none of yours, and this tardy letter from you shows that it is by no accident on your part but is your habit of mind.

What proves this to me is your reference to Bob "not getting any money out of the job, "while you Kaufmann and I are – say you.

Well if Bob is any good he is getting far more money out of it. In any case I would save you further anxiety on his behalf by reminding you that it is exactly none of your damned business no matter which way you may look at it. As for myself, I shall get so much less than money out of this house that I prefer not to be mentioned in that connection with Kaufmann and yourself.

When I sent for you I hoped to find real help in getting a difficult building built for a difficult client. But it seems to me now I sent for you only to find I have greater difficulty than either client or building in the man picked to be my right-banner. I saw "back down the line" as I read your brief and tardy and impertinent letter. As I learn what has happened to our plans and details as have been sent to Bob I see that I am in trouble.

I have therefore called Bob back here until some basis for mutual respect between myself and Mr. Kaufmann is reestablished. You are now included in this armistice if such it proves to be. If you imagine your meddlesome attitude to be either sensible or honest (we will not say ethical) something was left out of either your character or your education.

I have put too much into this house (even money, which item you will understand) to have it miscarry by mischievous interferences of any sort. The kind of buildings I build don't happen that way. Several have been ruined that way. And this one may be one of them.

It is only fair to say to you directly that you will either fish or cut bait or I will. I am willing to quit, if I must, but unwilling to go with my eyes open into the failure of my work. With a setup such as the present one turns out to be, there can be only failure. I have built one hundred and ninety of the world's important buildings without knowing the look of the thing when it turns up on the job.

Failure, I mean, by way of treacherous interference,
Sincerely yours,
Frank Lloyd Wright, Architect

Letter (7) August 30, 1936[lxv]
Mr. Edgar J. Kaufmann
Kaufmann's Department Stores
Pittsburgh, Pennsylvania

If your engineer was consistent in his checkup of our details he would have had to reject not only the reinforcement in the beams he questioned but through the building from start to finish – not only steel but concrete as well.

For this reason ... I have learned from experience with the earthquake proof Imperial Hotel and other buildings that the fiber stress in steel is safe at 25 and 30,000 lbs. and that the compression on concrete of 1,500 is entirely safe.

We have had those stresses in order to save you waste because we are not operating under contract conditions to meet the hazards of which the assumptions of your engineer were made. So why waste money to actually weaken structure by excess weight.

Also it had never been the practice of Adler and Sullivan with whom I served an apprenticeship of seven years [...] to assume a live load on reinforced concrete constructions in dwellings. By these assumptions we have not only saved you more than two thousand five hundred dollars but given you a stronger building.

Now if you had been above board in your dealings with your architect you might have saved your engineer from demonstrating his incompetence and saved your money as well. Incompetence because by applying the standards set for him he put his finger upon only two spots in the structure where sheer waste of standardized ignorance should be applied whereas he should have condemned the whole structure if he was consistent and reliable.

In interfering as you have you have set up a condition where we have no recourse but to accept an accusation that we do not know how to build our building without your help – and deliberately given current gossip a good break against us. Why? I thought I had found a man and a client.

But is this your usual method in dealing with men? If so I will make a prophecy – in ten years' time no one will work for you for either love or money.

I have worked for much of one in your case and little of the other. So damned little of the one (money) that it hardly matters in the consideration of the whole. And for this you hand me this betrayal to solve your own fear – if you were afraid why didn't you say so?

In short Mr. E. J. Kaufmann (client No. 199) these assumptions of your engineer, to wit: 750 lbs. for concrete – plus a 40 live load – 20,000 for steel would double the cost of your construction because not only is there double the cost of your structure but the increase to carry the increase in weight would be considerably more.

Now maybe these pearls of wisdom gained by experience have been cast before swine, and not only do the swine refuse to eat the pearls but turn and rend us.

What do you think? Does any client really know when he is well off?

Frank Lloyd Wright,

Architect

Letter (8) January 25, 1937[lxvi]

Dear E.J.:

I suppose there is nothing in your experience by which you might measure the disappointment t and chagrin which you have handed me. I have put [my] *best inspiration and effort into creating something rare and beautiful for you whom I respect and have conceived affection for only to find that so far as he could add ruin to my work and reputation he did so behind my back when I was helpless, with no idea, apparently, that he was so doing. Any pleasure I might take in having done something noble and fine for you is outraged by any outside interference with my effort on your behalf, no matter how well meant the interference may be. I think you are intelligent enough at least to get the idea. So let that pass.*

There is the work if art itself to consider [etc.]

The scare over the integrity of the structure is the usual exaggeration where such matters go. I have assured you time and time again that the structure is sound – but that I wanted no more check in parapets and was taking measures to avoid them. You took this doubtfully – and scared by Hall ran into the engineer's arms with it. Hall cannot explain to you why the parapet cracked. And Hall himself "crowned" nothing in the building as any experienced builder would have done to take up the inevitable 1" to 1-1/5" deflection in cantilevers and beams given in tabulations. As it is we have none. He can get away with it however. Your tests have not been tests at all but ignorant abuse.

Now I know the shortcomings of this architect as I know what to expect from his client [etc.]

Hall has now the thorough coaching he needed to go on further with his work. Bob Mosher has been working under my direction on the details necessary to complete the work and is going back with Hall to await your decision in this matter. Will you kindly hasten to give me the assurance for which I have every right to ask? So the work can go on to the successful conclusion for which we both ask?

Sincerely yours,
Frank Lloyd Wright,
Architect

Letter (9) (Undated) 1937[lxvii]

Frank Lloyd Wright, Architect

I hereby agree to do all in my power to see that the architect's instructions to the builder, Hall, or whoever may take his place, agreeable to the architect, are faithfully executed and that no exterior advice or criticism be allowed to interfere with the architect's authority over matters concerning the character and integrity of the building I have engaged him to build for me. And this is to continue until the building is completed to our mutual satisfaction.

Edgar J. Kaufmann, Kaufmann Department Stores, Inc.

Fallingwater's Challenges

Moisture Penetration

Most of the stone bearing walls of the structure have been designed to rise above the roofline. This was a decision dictated by the formal composition of the building's elevations. The horizontal ledges created by these walls and chimneys were relatively unprotected from moisture penetration. There was no coping details proposed for these surfaces. As a result, water was travelled through cavities inside the walls, eventually finding its way through skylights and floor slabs onto wall surfaces and into the building's interior space.

The grouting seal between stone pavers used in finishing the terrace floors were worn out over time and admitting moisture at greater rates than when first constructed. The rolled finish of the underside of the cantilevers and ends of ledges and overhangs provided surfaces on which precipitation ran down freely and onto exterior surfaces. The roofing overhangs had developed cracks and were unable to keep out moisture. Some of the skylights and windows were worn out by the humid climate of Bear Run, Pennsylvania.

The solutions to these problems meant considerable work ranging from surface repair to new moisture membrane installation within structural and non-structural elements. The architectural office of Louis Astorino and Associates was commissioned by Edgar Kaufmann Jr. to look into the moisture problems. Hence, the following work was done:

o The top coursing of stonework was removed from all of the protruding walls. Lead moisture barriers and flashing details (for chimneys) were installed. The stonework was replaced and restored to keep with the building's original appearance.
o Stone pavers on terrace floors were removed, and rubber membranes were installed.
o Broken off and cracked concrete surfaces were cleaned. Loose pieces were removed. Special round moldings were fabricated with pressured injection of concrete finishes onto these surfaces.
o Skylights windows and their frames were repaired and were replaced.
o Glazing was replaced with double glazing sandwiching a transparent membrane to reduce Ultra Violet Ray admission into the building.

In spite of all of this extensive work, given the heavy precipitation patterns found at this geographic region, this repair job is likely to be repeated in the future, hopefully in a more limited form. In dismissing roof leakage as a serious problem that often is not worth the effort expended at the outset, particularly in moisture laden regions like Bear Run Wright may have hit the nail on the head. It is conceivable that by taking such a position he was expressing architects' helplessness against nature's way with manmade structures

Structural Failure

The problem in this case was somewhat more difficult to diagnose. The sagging and cracking of the cantilevered slabs, which started almost immediately after construction and became progressively more pronounced as years went by, were just as critical a problem as the moisture problem.

Even though the compressive strength of the concrete used appears to be uneven, it is not below the stresses which were designed to be 3,000 lb/psi at a minimum. A culprit appears to be the omission of reinforcing tie-bars that connect the flow of stresses in the first floor cantilever beams to the *Pilotis* that support the cantilevers (Figure 13).

Robert Sillman Associates, a structural engineering firm, worked on this problem and its solution. They measured the deflection in the cantilever beams to be at 5-7 inches, which is excessive. The remedy in this case was post-tensioning of the cantilever beams to increase their tensile and compressive strengths as well as integrating the Pilotis with tie rods. This solution involved a problem of strategy. There were two possible directions from which the beams could be reached: from below and from above. The former required the removal of the stucco surface under the slabs; the latter the removal of the flooring inside the house. Engineers decided to remove the flooring since replacing the original external stucco surfaces would have been a greater breach of the design's authenticity.

They proceeded to label and mark the irregularly shaped flooring made out of fieldstone quarried from the region and access the cantilever beams. Once there, they post-tensioned the beams with rods taking care not to bend the sagging beams to avoid forming new cracks.

Exterior view of Crystal Palace, Hyde Park, London

Chapter 8 Crystal Palace: Design Expertise

Background

Sir Joseph Paxton (1803-1865), who was a self-made botanist, engineer, designer of greenhouses, and a recipient of Knighthood due to his accomplishments, created the Crystal Palace. This edifice housed the Great Exhibition of 1851, a world's fair of technology and industrial production. It was the largest international exhibition held anywhere in the 19th Century.

It marked the culmination of an extraordinary confluence of forces emanating from international politics, commerce, technology, and, architecture. Its impact on the design of buildings, not to mention the architectural world, is nothing short of remarkable. By some miracle of history, the first great exhibition glorifying modern industrialism was housed in a design, which more perfectly expressed its potentials than any that followed it (Figure 15).

The Great Exhibition of 1851, while a spectacular success in the end, did not start out with that promise. Primarily for political reasons, having been upgraded to the level of an ambitious international event, from that of a relatively small-scale national exhibition, suffered from a lack of advanced planning. This was particularly true in the case of the design of the building that was to house the exhibition. It was obtained at the last minute, at a time when all options were exhausted.

Figure 15: Main transept housing a full-grown tree, Crystal Palace, London

Figure 16: Modular facade of Crystal Palace, London

Even though a design competition was held that yielded more than 230 entries, the jury decided to use none of the submissions, including those that earned honorable mentions. As the jury, in a desperate move, was contemplating to assemble a hybrid design based on the features of some of the notable entries, Mr. Paxton was given a chance to submit a fresh proposal.

Paxton had started in the field of horticulture at the age of fifteen. In 1823, at the age of 20, he was employed by the London Horticultural Society to work on the Chiswick Gardens of the Duke of Devonshire. In this capacity, he was exposed to both field organization and techniques applicable to botanical and horticultural installations.

Eventually, he rose to the post of the Superintendent of the Duke's countryseat at Chatsworth. Throughout this time he nurtured his interest in the understanding of plants and organic life while building numerous structures in which rare plants were grown. He also traveled abroad and served as the editor of horticultural journals.

When Paxton was given the chance to design the edifice for the Great Exhibition, he was one of the most knowledgeable people anywhere about the construction of light structures and the supervision of their assembly. He found himself at the right time and place possessing just the right knowledge for solving the difficult design problem of the 1851 Great Exhibition. It can be said that serendipitously his entire life's work became relevant to the problem at hand.

Figure 17: Ridge-and-furrow installation system, Crystal Palace, London

Figure 18: Horse-powered winch lifts, Crystal Palace, London

In his earlier designs, he had perfected a unique glazing system, a variety of roof forms and spans with glazing materials, and a structural understanding of natural forms. Remarkably, his design for the exhibition was completed in eight days. It turned out to be the largest enclosure to date, boasting 989,884 sq.ft. of floor area and 1-1/2 miles of balcony space.

Owing to novel prefabrication and assembly technique Paxton devised, the construction was completed on time, within 26 weeks. It also responded to several important design criteria: such as, flexibility of use; lightness of structure; large spans; prefabricated assembly; integrated system of condensation and drainage; demountability; remountability; and a modular component assembly.

In no small way, did these accomplishment owe their success to Paxton's horticultural proves. During his long experience with botany, he integrated many design requirements of his greenhouse structures through an approach based on the leaf structure of the *Victoria Regia,* which he was the first person to cultivate in all of Great Britain.

Achievements of the Crystal Palace

Both in terms of design and construction the achievements of the Crystal Palace are quite remarkable. In addition to having the largest interior space of the day (Figure 15) it provided the most advanced vision for a structure designed to house world's most advanced technologies.

Not only was it modular for ease of assembly and reassembly; it also introduced standard manufactured details, complete prefabrication, systems integration and site assembly procedures with industrial efficiency, all of which signaled technology well beyond its time.

The building's modularly conceived and fabricated assembly was part of its original design consideration (Figure 16). Parts were manufactured off-site and shipped to site in the order of assembly, preconceiving the idea of fast-tract construction, which would only emerge a full century later.

These new approaches of construction at the site were absolute necessities for completing the work on time. Some prefabricated members were too large and heavy to put together with conventional methods. Rigs, which can be seen as predecessors of the modern construction crane, were developed (Figure 18).

A rail-cart called the Ridge-and–Furrow system was designed by Paxton to make glazing assembly more efficient (Figure 17). This cart was just large enough to carry a set of panes of glass and four workers. It fit exactly on the framing of the glazing system and used the framing as rails on which the carts moved. Once the construction was complete, these rail-elements served as gutters that channeled rainwater through downspouts that were strategically connected to underground storm water pipes, throughout the structure.

Not only in terms of advanced technology, but also in terms of spatial composition, Paxton's design predates some of the innovations that emerged only, in mid-20s, almost a century later.

Being a botanist by training Paxton was also motivated to save the natural flora of the site. This included large trees some of which in the end became indoor greenery adorning lofty enclosures, reminiscent of the modern atria of our day (Figure 15). Mezzanines surrounding these atria added a lofty sense of space throughout the building.

The most remarkable lesson that one can draw from the Crystal Palace is not the fact that these advances were conceived so early in the history of building design but how they were conceived at all. There is no easy answer to this question. Scholars studying the building converge around several points.

Due to his technical background, Paxton studied the problem with an *architectonic* point of view, creating novel forms based on building technology. He was able to adapt these methods that he knew intimately to the problem at hand. He happened to live at a time when new building materials, styles and techniques were emerging.

Ultimately, Paxton understood the challenges and limitations of novel designs and focused on finding innovative solutions. He also understood that if he were to overcome the challenges of timetable and budget, he would make his mark as an innovator.

There was very little room in his design schedule to refocus the problem so he just used what was available at the cutting edge of building technology. All he had time for was a single shot at a unique design, applied to a unique problem. He was also a consummate practitioner of the art of planning that was useful in managing so many innovations at once and completing design and construction within six months.

The End

In hindsight, the one thing that could have been but wasn't a part of the design requirements was fireproofing. The building was not fireproofed in the contemporary sense of that word, since at the time it was believed that a structure primarily made from iron and glass would not burn down.

This turned out to be a fatal assumption. After the conclusion of the world's fair the structure was demounted at Hyde Park, its original location, and remounted in the suburbs of London. Adapting its footprint and form to the new context, once again, reaffirming the building's innovative construction and design system.

At this new site, after a successful run as one of Londoner's most popular visiting grounds, the structure burned down in a brief and spectacular fire, in 1936, almost 85 years to the day after its original installation at Hyde Park. Today, we can study it only through the records left from its days of glory.

Critical Issues

Competitions are one of time-honored methods of acquiring commissions that happen to be notorious for their inefficiency, unfairness, and low probability of success. While they provide lifelong value to young architects as their first-time job opportunity, they also provide ample disappointment to many others who are eliminated from contention. This was the case for all competitors in the Crystal Palace competition – as well for hundreds in the case of the Sydney Opera House (Chapter 5).

Institutional Ethics identifies the governing of welfare and freedom of individuals as the most significant exception to moral conduct. It defines the basis of professional conduct as the avoidance of conflicts among the interests of sole proprietors.

In this case, there is a natural affinity with the Virtue-Consequence-Rights (VCR) trilogy of ethics frameworks that combine a range of criteria: namely the professional proprietor (in the domain of Virtue Ethics), the professional firm (in the domain of Teleology or Consequence Ethics) and the professional institution (in the domain of Deontology or Rights and Responsibilities Ethics), respectively.

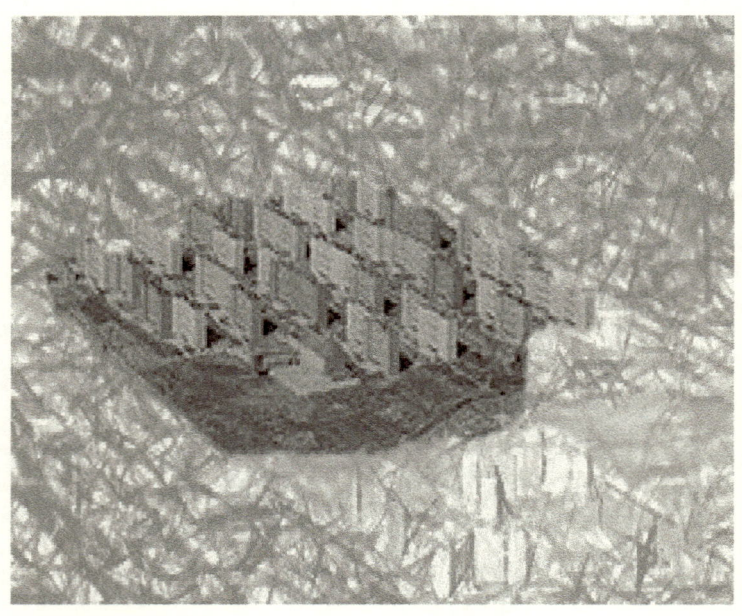

Aerial view of Pruitt-Igoe, St. Louis, MO

Chapter 9 Pruitt-Igoe: Nation's Conscience

This Chapter contains valuable input from several articles exploring the challenges of Pruitt-Igoe. We acknowledge three of them as key contributions to this subject; by Checkoway, B. (1985); Hoffman, A., and Montgomery, R. (1985).

The Pruitt-Igoe public housing project in St. Louis, Missouri, occupies a significant niche in the annals of architectural disasters. Designed for low-income families, the complex comprised 33 high-rise buildings, each of which being an 11-story structure; all together containing 2,870 apartments on 57.5 acres.

As with most "conventional" public housing that were built, owned, and managed by a governmental agency of the 1950s, Pruitt-Igoe was an example of one of the larger post-World War II slum clearance and urban renewal efforts, launched by a partnership between local municipalities and the federal government.

Often these efforts were aimed at the dilapidated, poverty-ridden slums of central cities where severe overcrowding and considerable deterioration of housing stock were prevalent. Consistent with this, most American public housing projects like Pruitt-Igoe tended to be built on urban rings within a few miles of central business districts.

It was hailed at its opening, in 1954, by the *Architectural Forum* magazine for its innovative cost-saving and community-building features (Figure 19). In slightly longer than a decade, Pruitt-Igoe came to be described by sociologist Lee Rainwater (1970) as:

"an embarrassment to all concerned...a household term...for the worst in ghetto living...no other public housing project in the country approaches it in terms of vacancies, tenant concerns and anxieties, physical deterioration."

By the early 1970's, rising maintenance costs, excessive vandalism, high vacancy rates, increasing crime, and a world-wide stigmatizing of the project resulted in a singular decision growing from a complex Decision Making process: Pruitt-Igoe had to be destroyed.

Figure 19: Community gathering at Pruitt-Igoe, early years

This ultimate act was preceded by an experiment in 1972 in which three of the buildings were demolished with explosives to test theories ranging from whether the structures could be efficiently razed, and the idea of conversion to low-rise structures. Lamentably, this image perpetuated Pruitt-Igoe's reputation as a failed project.

In reality, the remaining thirty buildings continued to stand mostly empty for several years until they were demolished during the summer of 1976; and not with explosives, but by the wrecking ball. In a final irony, the rubble from Pruitt-Igoe was trucked to a rock quarry in suburban St. Louis, adjacent to one of the most affluent communities in the US.

Figure 21: Limited implosion Pruitt-Igoe, late years

Idiosyncrasies of Public Housing

Several facts concerning public housing in the United States are essential to the understanding of problems that emerged in US public housing. Many of these facts arose from the basic premise that the free enterprise, capitalism prevalent in the US was resistant to governmental ownership and management.

Housing provided and owned directly by the government prior to World War II was confined to a relatively few thousand units intended for industrial workers and for disorganized experimental efforts to supply shelter for families in industrial centers during the Great Depression. By 1975, more than 40 years after the first housing program was inaugurated by the federal government, less than 2% of the nation's dwelling units were publicly owned and operated.

Following World War II, US faced severe housing shortages. Large-scale migration of rural workers to industrial cities during the war and reactivation of deferred "family formation," in the post-war period, produced overcrowding and demand for housing. In response to this, private industry built millions of single-family homes in the suburbs. Low down-payments and interest-rates, made possible by Federal Housing Administration, and a burgeoning post-war economy, facilitated a massive exodus from central cities to tract-housing in the suburbs.

In turn, this exodus was followed by new migration movements to cities fueled by whites and blacks of lower socioeconomic status abandoning rural farming communities in search of jobs, better accommodations, and the *American Dream* promised by the urban context.

During this post-war period, US embarked upon its first large-scale building program of public housing through a partnership between federal and local governments. This required a complex arrangement whereby the national government subsidized municipal housing authorities to purchase and clear deteriorated slum areas of central cities, thus ushering in the Urban Renewal movement.

In order to replace at least some of the housing destroyed in this process, the Federal Government also provided funds for local authorities to construct apartments for low-income urbanites. These buildings were to be owned, maintained, and managed by local agencies and financed by revenue from rent. The program, however, did not constitute a national commitment to provide housing for the poor. The goal of stimulating the economy and providing sufficient economic gains to the upwardly mobile and to enable them to enter the private housing market, remained.

Public housing was not intended for the poorest of the poor but for a group called the "deserving poor," who had at least some income and could afford a modest payment of rent. To facilitate this policy, maximum income standards were set, dictating that residents must move out when they achieved income beyond a threshold corresponding to that of the lower working class.

It is worth noting that the design of Pruitt-Igoe was based on what emerged from a prototype project called *Ville Radieuse* (Radiant City)[lxviii] designed by Le Corbusier, in 1950, for an idealized working class, albeit for the Algerian and European context.

Decline of Pruitt-Igoe

Pruitt-Igoe was the fourth public housing project undertaken by the St. Louis Housing Authority. "Originally conceived as two separate projects, one for blacks and the other for whites, the two were later combined "when the U.S. Supreme Court in 1954 invalidated the legal principle of 'separate but equal facilities' for the races."

At no time did the project enjoy an occupancy rate of more than 90%; and this level was maintained only for the first few years of its operation. During the 1960's the rate dropped precipitously, until by the end of the decade slightly more than one-third of the units remained occupied. Well before this time, the project had fallen into a state of severe physical decline and social deterioration, marked by excessive crime and vandalism rates (Figure 20).

Figure 20: Disrepair of fenestration, Pruitt-Igoe, late years

Less than six years after it was built, Pruitt-Igoe began to resemble a disaster area: *"a disgrace, a concrete ghetto, a 19th century caricature of an insane asylum."* [lxix] The federal department of Health Education and Welfare (HEW), in 1962, had committed over $5 million of its funds to Pruitt-Igoe in an attempt to alleviate the social problems associated with the project.

This money was to be used over an intensive four-year program of health, welfare, education, and rehabilitation. With the aid of this grant the Missouri state Division of Welfare established an office in the project and assigned a staff of 45 social workers to provide on-site services to the residents. A day-care center, health clinic, and other social facilities were set up; and a local university conducted a federally funded study of the tenants.

These efforts were accompanied by measures to improve the physical plant. Underwritten by HUD, $7 million was allocated of to renovate the project including general repairs, structural changes, installation of a new lighting system, and creation of picnic and playground areas. A carefully delineated action plan authorized by HUD and developed by the architectural firm of Skidmore, Owings, and Merrill, evoked little enthusiasm among community leaders. Doubts as to the economic feasibility of revitalizing the project were too strong to be overcome.

In 1970, because of the loss of tenants and the growing problems of security and maintenance, the Housing Authority vacated 27 of the buildings and moved the remaining residents into the other six structures. Three years later it voted to shut down the project entirely.

Shortly after, in August of 1973, the mayor announced that the City and HUD had reached agreement to raze all of the buildings. In making the announcement, the mayor said that the demolition would eliminate "*the terrible condition of Pruitt-Igoe and the stigma which its presence has brought upon our city.*"

Why the Failure?

Why did Pruitt-Igoe fail? Why did it become, as one newspaper commentator called it, "*the biggest nonmilitary fiasco in the nation's history.* " Conventional public housing in US has won only a few accolades. In fact, many Americans consider the program a failure. Yet in no instance have any of the nation's major projects become the physical and social disaster that was attributed to Pruitt-Igoe. Four sets of reasons have been advanced to explain this failure: (1) tenants; (2) design; (3) management; and (4) location.

Tenants

To some, the tenants were the major cause of Pruitt-Igoe's collapse. These observations included notions that the project was filled with unworthy and irresponsible tenants. Housing Authority statistics, to the contrary, indicate that Pruitt-Igoe residents did not differ greatly from those in the other St. Louis projects in terms of income, rate of employment, race, and percentage on public welfare. They do, however, show one significant deviation. Pruitt-Igoe from its inception exceeded the other projects in the proportion of female-headed families.

In 1956 it contained 30% of Aid to Dependent Children (ADC) mothers compared to an average of 15% in the others, and in 1960 the corresponding figures were 40% and 23%. Because ADC families tend to be large, Pruitt-Igoe's youth population percentage came to be substantially more sizable than that of its counterparts. Given the design of the complex, it's inadequate recreational facilities, and the general lack of job opportunities for teenagers, this factor may well have contributed to the high degree of delinquency in the project.

Design

Criticism has been directed at the design of Pruitt-Igoe and at the alleged insensitivity of the architects and planners to the needs of the people who were to occupy Pruitt-Igoe. The original plans, drafted by architect Minoru Yamasaki, called for a combination of garden apartments and high-rise structures at a density of 30 units per acre. For reasons of economy, this design was significantly altered.

At the insistence of federal authorities, low-rise buildings were eliminated and density increased to 50 units per acre. Higher than anticipated bid values were submitted that led to successive cutbacks. These cutbacks included reducing the amount of living space provided for each person, dropping virtually all landscaping, eliminating public restrooms at ground level (thus forcing youngsters to use stairwells and breezeways as substitutes), leaving the block walls of the stairways unpainted, failing to insulate exposed steam pipes, and cutting down the number of recreational facilities. As Meehan (1975) observed in his study of public housing policy:

ETHICAL DECISION MAKING IN ARCHITECTURE ● ÖMER AKIN

"The effort to reduce costs (in Pruitt-Igoe) focused heavily on those dimensions of the project which most directly involved the everyday life of the tenants and which were almost guaranteed to maximize their frustration and discomfort"[lxx]

Thirty-three buildings that comprised the complex were identical in design and were laid out in rows. Constructed of reinforced concrete faced with bricks, each building was organized around a single elevator and staircase in the center and stairwells at each end. Automatic skip-stop elevators opened only on every third floor, thus permitting a wide passageway or gallery, 11 feet deep by 85 feet long, to run across the front of the building every third floor. Architects came to envision these corridors as elevated neighborhood streets where tenants from the contiguous floors could congregate and small children play safely.

Imaginative as the notion of creating social enclaves within the buildings may have been, the galleries soon became havens for disruptive juveniles and muggers, gauntlets through which the tenants had to pass to reach their apartments. The windowless stairwells, which connected the floors to the galleries, created convenient settings for robberies, assaults, and rapes. What had been a design feature intended to enhance the quality of life for the tenants had within a few years become a nightmare.

Perhaps the most important casualty of the economic cutbacks was the standardizing of the living space size for all units regardless of the number of bedrooms they contained. This emphasis on small units proved to be a serious mistake, one that compelled larger families to crowd into already cramped quarters. As studies show, residential density measured by number of persons per room is correlated with indicators of social pathology.[lxxi]

Management

Management by the local Housing Authority has also been identified as a contributing factor to the project's decline. Its maintenance controls were inefficient and its relationships to the tenants generally poor. Yet its challenging practices were either imposed by federal guidelines or the result of factors over which the Housing Authority had little control.

One of the severe limitations imposed on Pruitt-Igoe was dependence on rent for income. Under the National Housing Act, the federal government funded only the cost of debt services, leaving the local agency to support all other costs out of rent income. It was not until 1969 that the Housing Act was amended to limit rent amount to 25% of tenant income, with the federal government making up the difference between it and the fair market price.

With full occupancy and a tenant population having sufficient income to pay economically viable rents, such a policy would have worked. In the case of Pruitt-Igoe, where neither of these two conditions were present, it had little chance to succeed. At no time after the first few years of its existence did the project produce more than 40% of the rental income needed. In addition, high maintenance costs, aggravated by vandalism undercut the solvency of the local Housing Authority that was compelled to raise rents, cut maintenance, and become less selective in screening new tenants.

Location

Located north of the principle axis of urban activity, in St. Louis, isolated from the main business district and major centers of industrial employment, and devoid of commercial activities, Pruitt-Igoe's physical decline was not anomalous. At the time the project was constructed, its surroundings, one of the oldest sections of St. Louis, was already in a state of physical decline. Most of the structures dated from the mid- or late-19th century, over two-thirds of them lacked adequate plumbing facilities, and nearly a third were overcrowded.

Crime rates were high and the area had long been a port of entry for migrants. During the late 19th and early 20th centuries white ethnic groups, principally Irish, German, and Italian, were the dominant occupants. Black families succeeded them in subsequent decades. By the time Pruitt-Igoe accepted its first tenants, the adjacent neighborhood was over 75% black.

In 1950, the one-fourth mile area surrounding Pruitt-Igoe contained 5300 housing units with an occupancy rate of 99%. By 1970 the number had fallen to slightly less than 4000, with only 75% of the units occupied, a trend that continued unabated. Some observers attribute this decline to the negative impact the Pruitt-Igoe had on its surroundings. Others argue that the neighborhood was already beyond salvation. Still others argue that the failure of the project was a reflection of the general conditions of the area in which it was located.

Critical Issues

Relevant Decision Making Models

Pruitt-Igoe presents a rich case of Benefit-Cost-tradeoffs in the capital delivery process, such as, poverty vs urban renewal, open-bid process vs contractor collusion, public funding vs local funding sources, and rental rates vs tenant availability. Due to associated risk factors, making smart choices within this complex environment was difficult.

Relevant Applied Ethical Frameworks

Social Justice is one of the foundations of morality. It strives to achieve fairness in all segments of society, especially the underrepresented and the underprivileged. The basic argument would be to establish equality based on rights not opportunistic tradeoffs.

In this context, the Pruitt-Igoe case vacillates between *Deontology,* where we have to protect the occupant's rights and responsibilities, and *Teleology,* where we need to look after the greater good above all else. It should not be a surprise to the observer of this case that decision makers tend to be torn between one framework and the next, often encountering gross violation of ethics regardless of which dominant framework is chosen.

Ethical Decision Making in Architecture ● Ömer Akin

Ethical Decision Making in Architecture
Part III: Methods
Ethics and Decision Making

Ludwig Wittgenstein

Part III Cover Image

Ludwig Wittgenstein (1889—1951)

He is one of the most influential philosophers of the twentieth century, and regarded by some as the most important since Immanuel Kant. His early work was influenced by that of Arthur Schopenhauer and, especially, by his teacher Bertrand Russell. This work culminated in the *Tractatus Logico-Philosophicus*, the only philosophy book that he published during his lifetime.

Part III   Methods: *Ethics and Decision Making*

Chapter 10   Architectural Decision Making

Chapter 11   Plurality of Ethics Theories

Chapter 12   Risk-Cost-Benefit Analysis

Chapter 13   Project Management: *Planning*

Chapter 14   Design Optimization

Fountain Sculpture, Silver Smith of Kutna Hora Castle, Czech Republic, by Ömer Akin

Chapter 10 Architectural Decision Making

The primary activities of architectural practice, at its highest level of granularity include project development, design, construction, occupancy, maintenance, and operations. Taken in this order, these also outline the typical workflow of building delivery. Architectural Decision Making is a key functionality in each one of these phases.

In the development phase decisions regarding location, scope, finances, schedule, aesthetics and marketing of a facility are primary. Some of the assumptions about the character of the design and the preferences of the designer are also determined at this time. These decisions lead to other decisions that are made during subsequent phases, such as massing, geometry, materials, construction techniques, and performance characteristics.

Once design decisions are completed, a "blueprint" for construction is at hand, which takes us to the next phase of decisions concerning scheduling, resource planning, management, and a myriad of site functions. Finally, when the construction of the facility is completed and commissioned to verify that it conforms to the design specifications, the owners and occupants take over, engaging themselves or their agents in the operation and maintenance decisions for the duration of the facility's life.

In this scenario, it is easy to see a server-and-served relationship between Decision Making and building. Architecture benefits from the methods and theories of Decision Making to undertake various tasks of design delivery; while Decision Making utilizes physical facilities as a domain within which to exercise its methods. Hence, we can define Architectural Decision Making as *"a collection of activities that facilitate decisions for the development, design, construction, maintenance and operations of facilities, using the theories, methods, and technologies available in the field of Decision Making."*[lxxii]

This is an atypical definition compared to what architects assume to be their purview. Decision Making is often considered to be an equivalent of design. That is, making all the necessary decisions to convert a given program into a fully specified physical design. Even at that, many designers regard this process something other than Problem Solving. [lxxiii] The intuitive and creative elements that are part of architectural design are generally regarded as creative processes that defy ordinary acts of Problem Solving.

The genesis of such impressions, or rather beliefs, can be traced back to the evolution of the profession of architecture. This evolution inscribes an interesting trajectory starting with the "Mechanical Arts," a notion in Antiquity and ending with the professional service provider notion of our day. Scholars of the Middle Ages, borrowing their disciplinary nomenclature from writers like Vitruvius, classified architecture under Mechanical Arts.

This is a category for "merely sensuous and exclusively manual arts" as opposed to "Liberal Arts" corresponding to Arithmetic, Music, Geometry, Astronomy, Grammar, Rhetoric, and Logic. As the latter continued to evolve into contemporary subjects of Mathematics, Physics, Chemistry, and Biology, that is, the sciences of our day, in its evolution, architecture remained in the "softer side" of the Mechanical Arts category. As recently as in the first half of the 19th Century, in most countries including the US, architecture was not even considered a professional field.

In 1804, while counterparts in Europe and England were beginning to enjoy significant rewards, Latrobe, one of the pioneers of the profession in the US wrote:

"Had I in England executed what I have here, I should now be able to sit down quietly and enjoy olium cum dignitate ... *Here I am the only successful Architect and Engineer, I have had to break the ice for my successors, and what was more difficult to destroy the prejudices the villainous Quacks in whose hands the public works have hitherto been, had raised against me"*

In terms of recognition and respect that they expected, it would take better than a century of concerted effort by US architects to make things right for themselves. A primary difficulty in this quest was the American way of life and the system of business, which encouraged pioneering practices.

At the turn of the 19th Century, building and town planning sectors were dominated by enterprising artisans and pioneering craftsmen who did not shy away from building houses as well as large facilities without legal sanctions or authority of a recognized profession. Rarely, if ever, were these practitioners properly trained. More than a quarter century after Latrobe's accounting, we see James Gallier, another Englishman in the US, a surveyor this time, making similar observations:

"The builders, that is, the carpenters and brick layers, all called themselves architects, and were at the time the persons to whom owners of property applied when they

required plans for building: the builder hired some poor draftsman, of whom there were some half dozen in New York at the time, to make the plans, paying them a mere trifle for his services. The drawings so made were, it is true, but of little value, and some proprietors built without having any regular plans. When they wanted a house built, they looked about for one already finished..."[lxxiv]

It was not long after this, however, that properly educated architects began to emerge onto the scene: including Charles Bulfinch, John McComb, Jr., Ithiel Town, A. J. Davis, Richard Upjohn, and Richard Morris Hunt. With this the architect's "image" was set into motion (Saint, 1983).

By distinguishing themselves from builders, namely the "villainous quacks," architects developed a new agenda for themselves based on the treaties of antiquity as well as current practices of the day: efficiency, safety, appearance, and economy.[lxxv] Naturally, each focus did not receive its just due from practicing architects.

For instance, Hunt the only *Beaux Arts* trained of the bunch championed the "extreme artistic" view to the detriment of the other objectives, in particular economy (MacKinnon, 1970). This ushered in the period of artistic excesses for the next three-quarters of a century. Coincidentally, this was synchronized with the emergence of an unflattering professional image for the architect as an irresponsible, unaccountable, poor excuse for a businessman. As late as 1970, researchers were detecting a certain disdain towards economics by those practitioners who were considered to be the most creative in the field.

During the next half century, Boston, New York, Chicago and, to a lesser extent, Philadelphia and Urbana, Illinois played important roles in the emergence of American Architecture (Table 4). These centers of urban and intellectual concentration were the venues where professional businesses, organizations, and educational institutions were founded.

H. H. Richardson, a student of Hunt, has been one of the most influential American architects emerging from this era. The firm of McKim, Mead, and White dominated architecture in New York through their large volume of work and flamboyant behavior. In Chicago, Adler and Sullivan and Burnham and Root benefited greatly from the "Chicago Revolution" which rebuilt the city after its Great Fire. Probably the two most influential architects that shaped our profession in the US came out of these two firms.

Adler and Burnham's agenda included three important items: developing effective rules for architectural competitions, registration of architects, and sharing in government commissions. They were instrumental in getting legislation prepared for architectural registration. Burnham entered a decade's long struggle with the US government in order to pass this legislation.

In 1897, with help of the newly formed School of Architecture at Urbana, Illinois architectural licensing succeeded for the first time in the US. By 1951, all 50 states passed licensing laws. Today, architectural commissions are assigned on the strength of professional ethics than that of legislation.

Table 4: Abbreviated chronology of significant events in the emergence of architectural profession in United States

Date	Event	Explanation
1804	Latrobe's comments	First trained architect
1820s	Charles Bulfinch in Boston	First architectural office in Boston
1820s	John McComb, Jr. in New York	First architectural office in NY
1829	Town and Davis in New York	First partnership
1835	Academy for the Fine Arts in NY	First professional organization
1848	New York Ecclesiological Society	Influential journal
1850s	Richard Upjohn	First ecclesiological architect
1850s	Richard Morris Hunt in NY	First Ecole educated architect
1857	American Institute of Architects	First chapter formed in New York
1865	Massachusetts Institute of Technology	First school of architecture in the United States of America
1870s	Rebuilding of Chicago: "the Chicago revolution"	Emergence of the high-rise and large architectural firms
1873	Burnham and Root	Influential Chicago firm
1881	Columbia School of Architecture	Second school of architecture in NY
1883	The Inland Architect and Builder	Influential Chicago journal
1881	Adler and Sullivan	Influential Chicago firm
1885	McKim, Mead and White	Largest practice in New York
1893	Tarnsey Act for government commissions	Legislation to enable architects obtain government jobs
1897	Licensing examination passed in Illinois	First legislation for licensing with help from school of architecture
1899	AIA office moved to Washington	Nationally recognized professional organization
1908	AIA raises fee scale: 5-6%	Opposed by politicians
1912	Commission of Fine Arts of the US government	Primary channel for commissions
1951	Passing of licensing legislation completed in all 50 states	Reciprocity between states not completed till 1970s

Commissions obtained from the government, including invited competitions, have traversed a long and arduous road. Today, government jobs are held to similar standards of the free market, with minor exceptions. Usually, complex restrictions are imposed on these projects by laws that govern the appropriation of funds. Also, various government agencies carry out their own in-house design and construction work eliminating many potential jobs for the open market. These problems are lessened to a certain degree due to the large number of registered architects who are employed in-house by these agencies.

Nature of Architectural Problems

Today, the US architect, along with engineers and other consultants, enjoys recognition as the lead professional in the assembly of complex facilities. To deal with the full range of decision areas, starting with development and ending with facility management, today's architect uses methods that are part of a professional legacy, i.e., intuitive design, as well as those that are a part of the formal set of Decision Making methods.[lxxvi]

This picture, conjoining the odd pairing of intuition and reason, raises interesting intellectual and practical tensions. When we have access to objective and quantifiable data, do we still need the intuitive methods? The answer is in the fact that design problems are framed unlike most other problems of building engineering. Primarily, design problems are characterized through the structure of three basic ingredients[lxxvii]:

P – Initial problem description

M – Solution methods

S – Acceptable solutions

Problems include a definition of the ingredients usually derived from the wants and needs of the client: pertaining to things like the building site, budget, functional requirements, and materials. *Methods* include various representation and investigation techniques used by the designer, particularly in generating alternative solutions to the problem at hand. These subsume knowledge shared by communities of designers, such as representation conventions, structural analysis methods, as well as specialized knowledge possessed by designers, including individual, even idiosyncratic, design strategies. *Solutions* include anything that would qualify as an answer the given problem, usually subject to selection criteria specifically defined for the problem at hand.

Then, the design process can be represented as:

P + M *yields* S   [1]

With this formalism, problems can be classified into two broad categories: *well-defined* and *ill-defined*.[lxxviii] A well-defined problem is one that has all three problem components, P, M and S, unambiguously defined at the outset. Prior to starting work on, say, a building design task, all of the relevant situational information relevant to the task must be at hand. In addition, at the outset, when such a problem is tackled, one has to have effective methods that can help in generating candidate solutions, as well as clearly stated criteria that can be used to accept or reject these potential solutions.

Conversely ill-defined problems, which are referred to through a variety of terms including "ill-structured," and "wicked," have one or more of poorly defined components of the formulation in [1] – either not defined at all, or volatile throughout the course of the design process. Often, problem circumstances and clients' minds can change faster than one can finalize the solution (Chapter 5). Particularly as they discover new information during their design processes, designers find room for new approaches to develop their designs and to construct their buildings. The criteria of acceptability can also change with the problem parameters. This is what is meant by the ill-defined-ness of architectural design problems (Akin, 1986).

How then do architects create a stable environment for making decisions? Simon, in his seminal work, *The Sciences of the Artificial* (1969), convincingly argues that ill-defined problems are converted into smaller well-defined, sub-problems. This is called Problem Decomposition. Once the well-defined problems are framed and solved, these partial solutions can be integrated into a holistic solution responding to the entirety of the original ill-defined problem. This is called Problem Recomposition.[lxxix]

While there is considerable research on the design process and its application in Architecture, professionals in the field are not eager to consider their trade in a "self-conscious" manner. They prefer to simply exercise their "art" rather than consciously thinking about the explicit thought processes involved. These issues fall under the "self-conscious view" of Architecture since they require going outside of the intuitive and un-self-conscious process of creation.

Ethical Decision Making in Architecture — Ömer Akin

This is a particularly difficult endeavor since architects are both very ambitious about the things they to do and also intentionally tend to sound tangential and ambiguous when asked to explain how they do it. A frequent quote from Le Corbusier's book, *Vers Une Architecture* provides an apt illustration:

> *"You employ stone, wood and concrete, and with these materials you build houses and palaces: that is construction. Ingenuity is at work. But suddenly you touch my heart, you do me good. I am happy and I say "This is beautiful." That is architecture. Art enters in. My house is practical. I thank you, as I might thank railway engineers or the telephone service. You have not touched my heart. But suppose that walls rise towards heaven in such a way that I am moved. I perceive your intentions.*
>
> *Your mood has been gentle, brutal, charming or noble. The stones you have erected tell me so. You fix me to the place and my eyes regard it. They behold something which expresses a thought; a thought which reveals itself without word or sound, but solely by means of shapes which stand in a certain relationship to one another.*
>
> *These shapes are such that they are clearly revealed in light. The relationship between them have not necessarily any reference to what is practical or descriptive. They are a mathematical creation of your mind. They are the language of architecture. By the use of inert materials and starting from conditions more or less utilitarian, you have established certain relationships which have aroused my emotions. This is Architecture."*[lxxx]

According to Le Corbusier, architecture is not the simple act of providing utility. It involves the creation of conditions that provide the satisfaction of needs beyond mere function. In his poignant definition above, Le Corbusier articulates these with greater skill than most. He, at once, establishes the value of satisfying utilitarian needs as well as the necessity of going beyond them; particularly if architecture is going to be worthwhile. He labels the former 'construction' and the latter 'architecture;' and calls the process that leads to the former "ingenuity;" and the latter "art."

Remarkably, these definitions also highlight the idea of architects being self-conscious about their tasks. In addition to establishing the criteria for which architecture, must be responsive, Corbusier argues that this is a particular creation of the architect's mind. He also indicates that this creation is a mathematical one; that it constitutes a language; and that all of this is revealed to the observer through thoughts and emotions. Each of these assertions is a part of the larger theme of the architect's self-consciousness and highlights the benefits of studying the architectural processes. In the end, it is fortunate that Le Corbusier's implicit and our explicit intentions merge in the self-conscious consideration of the design process.

Objections to the Self-conscious View of Design

There are, nevertheless, several objections to the idea of explicitly dissecting the Architect's thought process. One of these is based on the impossibility of the architect being cognitively conscious while in the midst of a demanding design process; let alone being self-conscious, about the process of creation. We shall call this the *irrationality* argument. It gives prominence to non-rational thought. Its premise is the belief that synthetic judgment as opposed to analytical and rational ones is inextricably connected to sensation and intuition that arises during the creative act.

Intuition is connected to both experiences and to concepts about objects that populate these experiences. The first part of this argument, which is about intuitive judgment, is prominent in Immanuel Kant's writings. In his seminal work, *Critique of Pure Reason*, he expresses this in its clearest form.

"In whatever manner and by whatever means a mode of knowledge may relate to objects, intuition is that through which it is in immediate relation to them, and to which all thought as a means is directed. But intuition takes place only in so far as the object is given to us ... Objects are given to us by means of sensibility, and it alone yields us to intuitions; they are thought through the understanding, and from the understanding arise concepts."[lxxxi]

In his search for the description of "pure" reason, Kant reviews forms of reasoning which constitute human thought in its totality. His delineation of these concepts shows that synthetic and analytic forms of reasoning differ from each other along the lines of experiential and *a priori* knowledge, respectively. Synthetic thought, through intuition, is connected to experiences and to concepts about objects that arise from experiences. This distinction appears to be fundamental and one that is echoed in various forms in the discourses about Architecture.

This brings us full circle to the primary objection to studying design thinking explicitly: "human cognition is a sub-conscious process and cannot be regarded consciously." The basic syllogism that supports this position goes like this:

- Design is an intuitive process;
- A significant portion of our intuition consists of subconscious thought;
- Subconscious thought processes are very difficult to study;
- Thus, the design processes are very difficult to study.

The second principal objection to the inquiry of architectural thought processes is that explicit descriptions of an intuitive process tend to "spoil" it. Architects can produce "genuine" pieces of work so long as they are not consciously thinking about how they should be doing this, or monitor their own actions as they are undertaking them.

The common analogy used is one of comparison to motor skills. Such as reasoning about the physics of one's motor behavior, as in riding a bicycle or walking a tight rope. This kind of reasoning is a hindrance to the task and not a help. Analogically, critics of Modernist architecture attribute the impoverishment of architectural detail and expression to the rationalist-functionalist attitudes promoted during Enlightenment and Internationalism to study design in a self-conscious manner. Kenneth Frampton writes:

"The success or failure of modern architecture to date, and its possible role in the future, must finally be assessed against [a] *rather complex background. In its most abstract form, architecture has, of course, played a certain role in the impoverishment of the environment - particularly where it has been instrumental in the rationalization of both building*

types and methods, and where both the material finish and the plan form have been reduced to their lowest common denominator ..."[lxxxii]

Frampton's comment offers evidence to expose the ill-effects of industrialization, functionalism, and minimalism, upon architecture. At least indirectly, he indicts efforts that attempt to expose the architectural design process. Although tacit in nature, such historical assessments are categorically anti-rationalist, since they are often used as arguments against reasoned and objective approaches.

These concerns, ordinarily, would be sufficient to discourage if not outright dissuade one from serious explorations of architectural cognition. First, there is the risk of not being able to penetrate the subconscious processes of the architect. Then there is the prospect of destroying the authenticity of design. The cold and indifferent conclusions of objective, rational, and preconceived processes may irrevocably alter our understanding of design for the worse. If by some chance these problems were alleviated, in order to unravel the intricacies of the architect's mind, we would still face the prospect of having to codify a large portion of intuitive reasoning, which is an overwhelming task, to say the least.

Motivation for Self-conscious Views of Design

Before we indulge in further pessimism about the subject of this chapter, and perhaps the entire book, let us recognize the potential rewards of the objective study of architectural reasoning, in historical, epistemological, and practical terms. First and foremost, modeling the reasoned process of Decision Making in design is central to a number of architectural movements that are considered important in the annals of architectural theory.

Starting with Classicism and the first known treaties of Architecture, the body of knowledge germane to it includes discussions of knowledge about the underlying thought processes of architecture. Vitruvius in his *Ten Books on Architecture*, for example, identifies two sources for the "*forms of expression in the arrangement of architecture:*" reflection and invention. Reflection is defined as "*careful and laborious thought, and watchful attention directed to the agreeable effect of one's plan.*" Invention, on the other hand, is the "*solving of intricate problems and the discovery of new principles by means of brilliancy and versatility.*"[lxxxiii]

In contradistinction to Kant's position on the value of intuition, there have been numerous credible efforts to understand subconscious and intuitive processes. In his treatise, even Kant shows how intuition can be isolated from all of the other thought processes and described in precise terms; thus refuting its inaccessibility. Since the Classical period, one can observe repeated and periodic re-emergence of the self-conscious formulation of architectural creation: including the Structuralism of the Gothic period, the Enlightenment, the Modern Movement as well as the practices of the present time.

Christopher Alexander in his seminal work *Notes on the Synthesis of Form* (1964) calls these moments in history "watersheds" implying a certain accumulation of intellectual inertia.[lxxxiv] Occasionally, such surges gave rise to fully fledged movements of erudition about understanding the mysteries of design cognition.

In Volume I of *Lectures on Architecture*, an influential treatise in shaping the broader impact of Enlightenment, Viollet-le-Duc, by pointing to the Cartesian Principles of thought, reemphasizes the importance of applying a rigorous method:

"It is therefore of essential importance to apply a rigorous method to this knowledge of the arts of the past; I do not know that I can do better in this matter than to abide by the four principles of Descartes, and which he deemed sufficient, 'provided' he remarked, 'that I made a firm and constant resolution not to neglect them in a single instance.' "The first" he, adds, *"was never to receive anything as true which I did not clearly know to be so.. The second, to divide each of the problems I was investigating into as many portions as possible, or as should be requisite for a complete solution. The third, to follow a certain order in my thoughts, beginning with those objects which are simplest and most easy to understand,... The last, to make such complete enumerations and general reviews in every field of inquiry as that, I should be certain of omitting nothing."*[lxxxv]

Once this topic is broached, and the veil of taboo draped over the exploration of the subconscious is parted, inquiring into the subject matter is unavoidable. Alexander (1964) calls this the loss of innocence. Whether we stand for or against pure intuition, we must do so with explicit reason.

"The use of logical structures to represent design problems has this important consequence; it brings with it the loss of innocence. A logical picture is easier to criticize than a vague picture since the assumptions it is based on are in the open. Its increased precision gives us the chance to sharpen our conception of what the design process involves. Once

what we do intuitively can be described and compared with non-intuitive ways of doing the same thing, we cannot go on innocently accepting the intuitive method."

Finally, there is the critical shortage of scholarship on the topic of architectural Decision Making. Works dedicated to Decision Making are normally directed towards non-architectural disciplines, such as Philosophy, Political Science, Economics, Management Science, and Computer Science. Here, we are attempting to add architecture's fair share of knowledge to this larger domain. Since architecture involves the intuitive as well as the rational process, in addition to knowledge about specific domains of construction and open-ended ones about the social and cultural attitudes of users, the scope of this enterprise is open ended.

Concepts such as the *Sciences of the Artificial*[lxxxvi] promise to initiate this enterprise that we may want to call Sciences of Design. We will cover this terrain in several chapters in this section. First we will consider well-defined methods for well-defined sub-problems of design, including Plurality of Ethics Theories, Cost-Benefit Analysis, Planning, and Optimization.

ETHICAL DECISION MAKING IN ARCHITECTURE ● ÖMER AKIN

Old Town, Prague, Czech Republic, by Ömer Akın

Chapter 11 Plurality of Ethics Theories

The handful of frameworks and ethical theories covered in the earlier chapters do not represent the entire picture of ethical diversity. One can argue that an inclusive set of frameworks are potentially too numerous to list if not virtually endless in number. One practical accounting includes sixteen major frameworks (Table 5), which is not an exhaustive list. Nevertheless, it is a good starting point to understand the notion of *plurality* and strategies needed to deal with it.

Assuming that for each framework included in Table 5 there could be any number of versions, each of which would present significant advantages and disadvantages for conducting ethical adjudication. Furthermore, where one framework indicates a course of action in one direction another one may well point in the opposite direction. Let us consider a hypothetical case to illustrate

By some accident of fate, Professional A and Professional B, cohorts on a cruise, survive a tragic capsize by climbing onto a lifeboat. Enduring a life and death struggle with the ocean and the sharks, they manage to reach a deserted island. Professional A has been hurt during this ordeal with the sharks and senses that the end is near. He shares with his friend Professional B his last wish and testament: "please donate my millions to the Ville Radieuse *movement." Professional B agrees. Professional A dies. As luck would have it, Professional B is saved by a passing freight carrier and lives to realize his promise to Professional A.*[lxxxvii]

Table 5: Sixteen alternative ethical frameworks[lxxxviii]

Framework	Brief Description
Deontology	principle of observing individual/institutional rights and responsibilities in the context of rival choices.
Teleology	principle of comparing the results of rival actions
Utilitarianism	principle of judging rival courses of action on the basis of their utility to the constituents engaged in it
Situational Ethics	assessing rival courses of action on the basis of the specific situation within which they apply
Virtual Ethics	assessing choices in the simulated setting of interests that mimic the real situation
Values	principle of comparing rival alternatives on the basis of human values
Legality	using laws and similar legal tenets to determine right from wrong
Policies / Codes	using institutional and societal policies and codes to determine right and wrong
Honesty and Integrity	a limited version of the Aristotelian *Virtue Ethics* that hinges on two human virtues as the lynch pin of choosing between alternative courses of action
Benefit/Harm Test	a less complicated version of Teleology where the chosen alternative must be shown to have more benefits than harms
Equality	making choices in which the options are weighed using the principle of equality of individuals influenced by the choices
Justice	principle of observing that the choices render just results for all involved
Rights	principle of observing that the choices do not violate individual's rights to life and well-being.
Kantian Ethics	principles that the right moral rules are those which individuals would freely choose to have govern them and always treating persons as ends-in-themselves and never merely as means to your ends
Conscience	litmus test of one's conscience to determine the correctness of a course of action
Public Scrutiny	putting the action of choice to the test of public knowledge

It turns out that *Professional B*'s choices can go in two very different directions:

o   *Scenario 1*: Disenchanted with the poor results of the *Ville Radieuse* movement in urban renewal projects in the US, Professional B can decide to dedicate the millions to the cause of low-rise, New Town projects.
o   *Scenario 2*: Alternatively, Professional B can decide to donate the millions to Professional A's friend Albert Speer, who has recently embarked upon projects for the Third Reich.

What do we make of *Professional B*'s choices? Is he justified to renege on his promise because he believes that the low-rise New Town developments have a better chance of succeeding than the elevated cities of three-million inhabitants? If so, then why would we see anything wrong with his acting on the belief that Speer is also onto something really big for the field of architecture?

The act of reneging (in both scenarios) is obviously on a collision course with *Virtue Ethics*. Loyalty and friendship would compel us to observe a promise we make to a friend, particularly on his deathbed. Similarly, *Honesty and Integrity Ethics, Values Ethics,* and *Kantian Ethics* would direct us to observe our promise without alteration. *Teleology, Utilitarianism, Situational Ethics,* and *Benefit/Harm Ethics*, on the other hand, would recognize the new emerging trends and encourage us to reassess the situation. Can the gains to be realized by the potential beneficiaries of these scenarios be justified?

Let us explore this by considering some of the framework listed in Table 5.

- Under *Justice*, oriented towards public's interests, *Professional A*'s preferences for the *Ville Radieuse* movement, as interpreted by *Professional B*, are in conflict with architects' mission to serve the public.
- Under *Deontology*, *Professional B* should be torn between two responsibilities, one towards his friend *Professional A* and the other towards his obligation, again as an architect, to the public.
- *Deontology, Rights, Conscience,* and *Public Scrutiny* ethics should direct *Professional B* to either conclusion.

The act of contributing to the Third Reich (Scenario-2) on the other hand may be more clearly adjudicated. Since the outcome of Speer's architectural and other exploits under Hitler's leadership are known to us in hindsight, we would lean towards condemning this action. Yet an assessment with the knowledge of what will happen in the future is not proper adjudication. Since decision makers should be innocent of knowing future consequences of choices, we cannot hold them responsible for making incorrect ones.

An objective exploration devoid of such assessments can well lead to a similar split decision as is the case in Scenario-1. On the grounds that new knowledge would be gained, *Situational Ethics* may justify the decision, while the *Conscience Ethics* may oppose it since Speer's architectural experiments serve a regime which places millions of human lives at risk.

The ultimate lesson we take away from these considerations is that ethical frameworks are: (1) multiple, (2) in potential conflict with each other, (3) direct us to understand morality from others' points of view, and (4) point to the value of reaching negotiated outcomes between participants.

In order to manage the plethora of Ethical Decision Frameworks, some of which we briefly considered here, we need specialized tools and methods that can make the adjudication problem tractable.

Peter Madsen[lxxxix] has proposed an approach that does just that: *Ethical Pluralism*. In this approach, we are not allowed to make assumptions about others' interests. We are compelled to consult them directly about the benefits and harms that they consider most important and the principles of morality that they hold supreme. Consequently, we need to assemble all constituents of a case in one space, around a physical or virtual table; give a say to all interested parties whether they are empowered by politics, wealth or status, or not; and make these proceedings fair to all by taking into account all points of view.

Such an exchange would take the form of negotiation through the empowerment of all. There are obvious pros and cons of this strategy, Some point out the difficulty of being all inclusive and assembling everyone in one location to negotiate and debate the best or most ethical course of action. And, others argue that this approach closely resembles the *Situated Ethics* framework and therefore does not deserve special disposition.

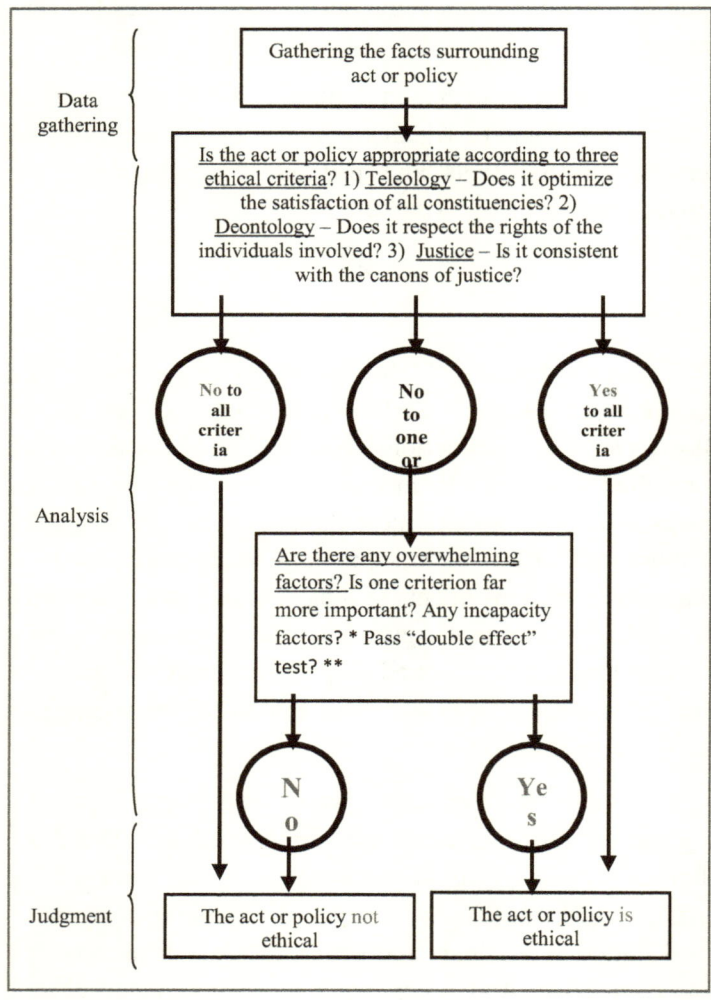

Figure 22: Ethical Adjudication Tool by Cavanaugh

A Rational Approach to Adjudication

In Figure 22, we consider a method, while more didactic in its approach that provides a practical solution and potentially greater certainty in its results (Cavanaugh, 1984). This method is a specific decision tool to help adjudicate with relative certainty when one has a limited number of ethical frameworks to consider. To illustrate, let us consider three potentially divergent frameworks: Deontology, Teleology, and Justice (Figure 22).

First, we take each framework independently and attempt to find a resolution based solely on that singular framework. Then we enter the results of each framework's analysis into the decision flow shown in Figure 22.

If all decision paths agree in favor of one course of action, say to donate the millions to Albert Speer, then the decision-"yes" will be selected by unanimous consent. If all agree against this course of action, then the decision is a unanimous-"no." When there is disagreement, the decision box in the middle is used. In this case, there are three additional considerations used to break the tie.

o *Is one criterion far more important?* For example, one might consider the benefits to the architectural community, however important they may be, would pale in comparison to the potential harm to humanity.
o *Are there any incapacity factors?* Incapacity factors render a criterion ineffective due to lack of sufficient information or inability to predict consequences. We may be in fact unable to assess if a donation to Speer's architectural experiments would have any effect on the Nazi cause. We may speculate that it would or not do any significant harm or good; but this does not change

the fact that we simply would not know for sure. This weakens our confidence in that choice.

- *Does it pass the test of a double effect?* Double effect is to say that the good consequences of an action should outweigh its bad ones. If this cannot be shown, then the test is not passed. Each course of action may have both good and bad consequences. We can argue that whatever benefit Speer's experiments would result in, they would not exceed the damage caused by the Nazi party and therefore would not produce any appreciable benefits.

After evaluating each option we can see towards which framework the weight of the final choice is leaning. If in the end there is still a tie between the options then our recourse is to gather everyone around the Plurality Table.

ETHICAL DECISION MAKING IN ARCHITECTURE ● ÖMER AKIN

ETHICAL DECISION MAKING IN ARCHITECTURE ● ÖMER AKIN

Wildlife at Erhai Valley, Yunnan Province, by Ömer Akın

Chapter 12 Risk-Cost-Benefit Analysis

Risks

The concept of risk in Decision Making is less associated with the notion of hazard and more related to the likelihood-value of a choice. However small it may be, every time we make a decision we run the risk of selecting the wrong choice. Mapping this notion into a general theory of Decision Making requires that we measure the expected risk that would result from the alternative choices available to us. Since each measurement can potentially yield a very small number as well as a large one, the aspect of hazard or the lack of it has to be represented as the magnitude of the value of the risk.

There is an intuitive example of thinking about risk. Marsh and McLennan Companies, asked the public if they considered life in the 2000s to be more risky than life in the 1980s or the 1960s. They found that corporate executives considered 1980s about as risky as 1960s. Federal regulators, members of congress, investor-lenders and the overall public considered the same risk differential to be greater than 20% for 2000s, 47% for 1980s, and 72% for 1960s.

As shown in this study, assessment of risk does not have to be entirely subjective; it can be quantified. We can also measure factual events such as the likelihood of death as a function of past trends. In 1900 the death rate for children between 5 and 14 was 4 per thousand, per year. In 1975 this rate dropped to 0.4 per thousand, per year. We can simply deduce from this that the risk of death in 1975 was reduced tenfold (Doll, 2002). This kind of reasoning is called *Bayesian Logic*.

In building industry decisions, we can consider a variety of real or hypothetical risks. The likelihood of (*Item 1, below*) a first time client liking a design, (*Item 2, below*) the engineer completing the structural design by a given deadline, (*Item 3, below*) the structure collapsing before its first year of occupancy, or (*Item 4, below*) getting paid adequately for a design can all imply risks. We can assign odds for these items based on past experience.

(Item 1) Odds of 50-50 with the average client - The interesting aspect of each of these cases lies in the degree of confidence we can assign to each judgment. The architect has as good or as poor a chance with the average client, therefore there is a 50-50 chance of convincing them about the goodness of their design. This is not because she knows the odds to be so but because she does not know enough about any clients' likes and dislikes. Hence, risk assignment is sometimes based on the absence of knowledge rather than the presence of known risk.

(Item 2) Odds of 80-20 for an average engineer-architect team - Mostly, deadlines by design consultants are met about 80% of the time. This is, at best, an educated guess and it may or may not hold in every case. However, poll takers and statisticians would assure us that given a sufficient number of tries this would be a reliable planning benchmark.

(Item 3) Odds of 85-15 for the Citicorp building, in 1978 - In the case of the Citicorp building we know that after its construction the likelihood of disaster was estimated to be about 15% each year it was spared a disaster. This was a matter of certainty.

(Item 4) Odds of 0-100 in the opinions of most architects - And finally, the 0-100 odds, as subjective as it may be, refer to architects universally valuing their work more than what they actually earn in monetary terms.

In conclusion, it is critical to qualify risk as a function of a numerical probability of occurrence plus the applicability of that probability to the case at hand.

Costs

Once the risk associated with an event is understood, next we must understand the cost associated with the risk, or the consequences of the likely event. The cost of a client rejecting a preliminary design is a lot less critical than a 56-story building collapsing. With additional work a missed deadline can be corrected, just as a rejected design can be revived; but the perception that a design is undervalued remains a fundamental problem for the entire architectural profession. The cost of fixing each case is different and risk analysis needs to take this into account.

It is important to recognize that the cost of solving such problems means reducing the associated risk to acceptable levels. Odds of 50-50 to gain the client's approval may just be fine for the average architect. They know that repeated tries are necessary; and a good designer learns with iterations. Furthermore, the cost of improving this outcome may be just as difficult as getting rid of the *Undervalued Syndrome*. It is safe to assume that the odds improve with the architect's years of experience, and self-selection exercised by clients and architects.

The cost of the delayed project and the collapsed building cases can be more accurately estimated, although estimating the loss of life in a collapsed building, in monetary terms, can invite fierce disagreement. While the former represents an insignificant fraction of the latter, there are cases in which the two factors are inter-connected. Time-pressures lead to fatal design errors and detection of serious flaws can delay a project for years.

Benefits

Without an understanding of the benefits of reducing the risk in a given situation there can be no valid Risk-Cost-Benefit analysis strategy. In the field of practice, these likelihoods represent relatively stable values. Effort and payoff are independent variables that must be taken into account while making decisions on other factors such as estimating completion time, requesting fees for services, which are the *dependent* variables.

When the costs and benefits are commensurate, the reduction of risk is not only desirable but also feasible. The cost of the building collapse risk is so high that regardless of the feasibility of risk-reduction it must be achieved. It also turns out that the entire discipline of engineering has been geared towards this goal. Building codes, professional licensing procedures, design safety factors, and a myriad of checks and balances established in design delivery, are intended to make sure that such risks never rise above acceptable levels.

Once a comprehensive risk analysis, including associated costs and benefits, is in hand, the logical next step is to conduct a benefit-cost estimate. This foresees a comparison of the costs and benefits to determine the means through which risks can be reduced to acceptable levels. The difficulty of solving a problem of risk-reduction and the magnitude of its probability can determine the path to a solution. The difficulty of solving a problem of risk-reduction is the key challenge in risk management.

Highly likely events like the possibility of demolition or recycling of a building within the time frame of, say, 100 years, such as in the case of the Crystal Palace, would invite *risk prone* behavior and are best left outside of the scheme of risk-planning. Inversely very unlikely events, like that of a 500 year hurricane hitting the Atlantic coast, as was the case for the Citicorp building in New York, would invite *risk averse* behavior and not constitute extraordinary design criteria.

Finally, benefits to be gained, regardless of the cost, can be justified as a legitimate decision strategy. Saving one day in the schedule of three years of design, as in the case of the Sydney Opera House, would hardly move the designers to change their course of action. On the other hand, insuring the safety of occupants is always sufficient cause for recalculating the structural design especially if the fee for doing so has already been provided, as in the case of the Kansas City Hyatt Regency.

ETHICAL DECISION MAKING IN ARCHITECTURE — ÖMER AKIN

Details of the *Nationality Room,*
at the *Cathedral f of Learning*, by Ömer Akin

Chapter 13 Project Management: Planning

Planning is the Decision Making method par excellence. It is the activity that helps imagine tomorrow, today. Designers are planners in the spatial domain. They make visual, analytical, and quantitative plans, to create objects that yet do not exist. Furthermore, and often implicitly, they make plans for actions to be executed: drawings to be drawn, models to be built, meetings to be held, material to be moved in order to create planned assembly at the site. Some of these plans are implicit in the drawings made.

The working drawings may show a bridge being designed in its entirety, while the construction sequence would start with the foundations and then move to the bridge structure. Usually these are implicit sequences of actions not evident in the drawings. The general contractor or builder has the unenviable task of inferring them correctly or conferring with a myriad of designers, so that they can, in turn, make their own plans-of-action. If for example the bridge to be built needs to be pre-fabricated, the construction sequence may start at the factory, not on the site; and with the upper structure, not the foundations.

Good planners develop ideas about how they should proceed throughout their planned activity. They define goals, sub-goals, and recursively breakdown their tasks into discrete acts that can be carried out without cognitive overload and likelihood of retracing steps of execution. However this introduces a plethora of decisions managed by dozens of technical personnel and decision makers often distributed over large geographic terrains.

This creates a natural flux of decisions, decision changes, and owing to the dependencies between these decisions, multiple cycles along the lines of dependency. Planning a goal hierarchy through which the complex problems are decomposed into discrete and well-defined parts is the principal planning strategy. This invites a series of questions.

- What methods should be used to successfully plan and execute these strategies?
- What methods should be used to manage budgets and schedules of these projects in the face of expanding tasks and responsibilities?
- What methods should be used to prevent functional shortcomings of the final product, which may result from the sheer impossibility of fully verifying and validating design strategies and intentions?

To address these questions let's consider the various levels of design Decision Making through the anatomy of a typical practice. This anatomy consists of three concentric levels: (1) *Top Level*: larger context of the design; (2) *Middle Level*: design team; and (3) *Low Level*: individual designer. Let us visualize these as concentric circles where the designer is nested inside circle of the design team, which in turn is nested in the larger design context (Figure 23).

In the outermost Context Level, we model the domain of the client, owner, user, financier, developer, official agencies, and general public. Here, the design team is just one of the agents interacting with the others, who are subject to external influences and constraints. These external influences include zoning ordinances, budgets, and the social-cultural context of a design.

Coordination is the *modus operandi* of the top or Context Level. In current design literature, coordination involves processes described as "concurrent engineering" in which several domains of design converge to resolve the design problem. Since universal standards for building products and processes do not exist, Case-Based Reasoning (Kolodner, 1993) is prevalent to a great extent, particularly when the facilitation of communication between many agents is necessary.

Commonly known cases provide the benchmarks and prototypes for the coordination of products and processes. Reliance on such prototypes can eventually lead to efficient production of designs, design standards, case-based tools, improved building codes, and requirement modeling techniques.

Standardization efforts have been going on for decades, such as those by the International Standards Organization (ISO) that have paved the way to substantial progress in the building sector. Industry Foundation Classes (IFC)[xc] is one of the current darlings of this sector. It is hoped that standards such as IFC will eventually take out the wrinkles in building product communication.

The Middle Level, in the three-level model shown in Figure 23, is the design team's domain. Here, the project representation that is dynamically maintained by the active participation of a homogeneous group of agents reside. Yet each member of this group views the design process somewhat differently; depending on their area of expertise (structural, mechanical, traffic, construction, and so on).

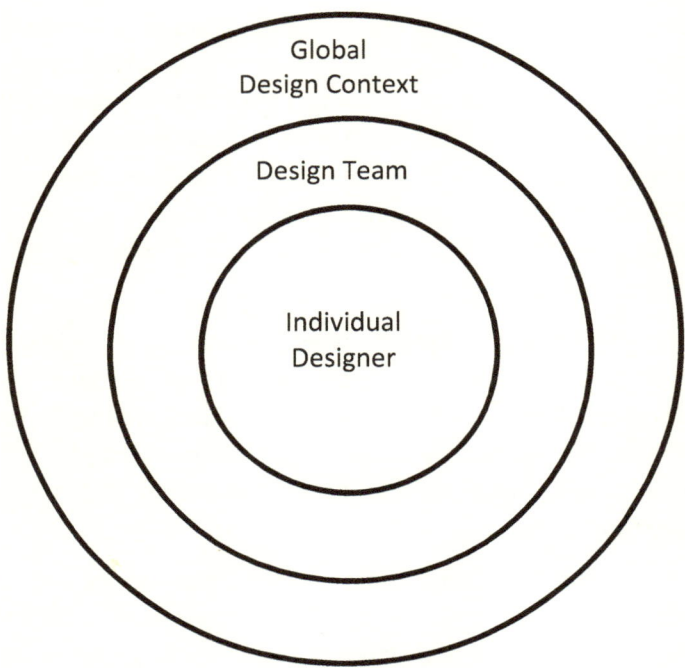

Figure 23: The concentric relations between the context, the team and the individual.

Together, they bring their concerns and solutions into one representation and solution through *negotiative* reasoning. This is much like the process conducted at the Context Level, where its dynamics follows the coordination of components in the define-execute-repeat cycle. Negotiation is the art of diplomacy, at best, and the art of role playing, at worst. Agents and groups have specific goals and expectations. They assume postures that take into account the roles and expectations of other agents in order to insure that each will succeed with their own set of goals.

This kind of interaction can be illustrated through *power games*[xci] that define the relationships between developers and designers, where developers typically look after the bottom line and designers largely care about design quality. Some patterns of behavior are prototypical and coordination mostly relies on negotiations that are conducted through informal and unpredictable ways.

The lowest and the innermost level of our model in Figure 23 represent the activities of the individual designer. Here, the typical *structure-solve-repeat* cycle prevails. Functions of this domain are typically characterized by two modalities: representations directed at the *internal*, cognitive world of the designer and representations directed at the parameters of the *external* context of the design.

The critical avenue of investigation at this level is to create powerful representations in both modes. In the internal modality, much has been accomplished in helping visualization and graphic rendering of physical objects. However, the methods in this area are still inadequate in providing high-level, intuitive IT techniques that come natural to the designer.

In the external modality, even less has been accomplished. Most design decisions require textual, computable, and semantic information outside of the visual domain. Design requirement specification, evaluation, and tracking are elusive targets for digital design systems.

As the complexity of designs increase so do the difficulties in this area. Research in computational processing of the graphic as well as non-graphic views of design affords the best promise for progress in this direction (Akın and Özkaya, 2007).

Scope of the Project Management Process (PMP)

Project management according to the Project Management Institute, is:[xcii]

"... the art of directing and coordinating human and material resources throughout the life of a project by using modern management techniques to achieve predetermined objectives of scope, cost, time, quality and participation satisfaction."[xciii]

Generally, project management is distinguished from the management of corporations through mission-oriented strategies. In this case, project organization is terminated when the mission is accomplished.

At the highest levels, the states of the Project Management Process (PMP) operate through a tacit agreement between the agents who are responsible for the construction administration, working drawings, design development, and schematic design. Akin (1993) in a research project studying the PMP in several national and international architectural offices found that within each phase there are critical states which significantly impacted the course of the overall design process.

These states have been categorized under two major headings, pre-contract and post-contract, based on structural and functional characteristics of the PMP. The pre-contract states belong to a phase during which the client and the firm consider the architectural problem in order to define the precise parameters of the work. The post-contract state, while more involved in terms of agents and roles played by them is not a phase during which parameters are defined. It is in this phase that those agreements formed earlier are carried out.

The role of the pre-contract state appears to be to insure the mutual satisfaction of both the client and the architect with the scope of the task at hand:

a) Identifying the limits of the solution domain.
b) Developing the conceptual design for the project (form, style, organization).
c) Involving non-architects (i.e., the client) in decisions
d) Negotiating rather than organizing the decision making process.
e) Backtracking of decisions and basic assumptions, based on need.
f) Communicating with the client about what is and is not desirable.

Once the parameters of the commission (cost, schedule, and product) are determined in the pre-schematic stage, the post-contract stage completes the delivery process. This includes:

a) Completion of the documentation of the building and the building itself.
b) Decisions taken internally without the involvement of the client.
c) No backtracking allowed to the earlier conceptual design stages.
d) Decisions by experts limited to their specific areas of expertise.

Models of Architectural Project Management

Project management in architecture has been considered an instance of management in general. As evidence is gathered through architectural case studies and comparisons of data between architecture and other application areas, a more heterogeneous picture has emerged. Depending on the specific circumstances of each practice, such as the job, building type, client, or economic context, management practices differ.

Based on a survey of practices in nine medium to large architectural offices (Akın, et.al., 1996), management practices were studied through specific project inventories, in-depth interviews and a complete set of project documents, including meeting notes, official and unofficial correspondence, and technical documentation specific to particular project types.

The method of analysis used was based on Information Processing Theory[xciv] with the intent to show the relationship between structural aspects of office organization and functions required to complete projects.

The findings indicate correlations between management practices and the definition of *service quality* by the firm and the individuals in the project teams. The findings of this study indicate three specific approaches to architectural project management: *Project Based, Matrix Based* and *Migration Based* models.

Project Based

Firm-7, the best representative of the Project based model in which the structure of the team was strictly hierarchical, a managing principal served as the team leader.

The project manager and a crew of production team members served under his or her direction. The principal was responsible for all decisions, contacts and negotiations with client and external consultants. A job captain served under the principal in coordinating the required tasks and managing the technical and drafting staff. This format is typical of small, high style design firms that are sought after because they provide strong design ideas, and a traditional, practice-centered business model.

Matrix Based

In Firm-3, the situation was quite different. Here all top level personnel remained more or less uniformly engaged in the project. The split of responsibility in this case was laterally organized, as opposed to the vertical organization of Firm-4 (the Migration Based model, discussed below). A principal was in charge who managed the entire job. The project team consisted of up to three sub-teams working with three project designers, each responsible for a different aspect of the project: interiors, space planning and exterior skin. The leader of one of these sub-teams also served as the job captain and the project manager who coordinated the entire project. During the delivery process, the central support staff facilitated the work of all teams for every project going through the office.

Migration Based

Firm-4 was a relatively small, 26-employee office with considerable diversity in the services provided. It was a full-service architecture and urban design firm which was also involved in sizable urban and regional development projects. One of the ways Firm-4 maintained its relatively small size and versatility is through a series of innovative management practices developed in-house. It was set up to *migrate* employees from one project to another based on a weekly scheduling activity undertaken by managing principals.

The firm's set up provided maximum flexibility for the managing principals, one for design and the other for management, in allocating individual staff members to tasks. This is the basis under which employees were hired and retained. This degree of interconnectedness and flexibility also afforded the firm the ability to organize its project team almost in the manner of a relay team. Employees assumed duties and major responsibilities that phased in and out as some other employee's duties and responsibilities did the reciprocal moves. In this way, each stage of the PMP was directed by an individual whose expertise was best suited to that design project.

The functions performed by all firms had certain similarities. All jobs were full service jobs starting with programming and ending with construction supervision. The collection and distribution of information as a result of the organizational patterns used in each case seemed to influence the success of some key functions of the PMP.. Some of these practice patterns shed light on the role of CAD in design management and on the differences of management for quality of service.[xcv]

ETHICAL DECISION MAKING IN ARCHITECTURE ● ÖMER AKIN

ETHICAL DECISION MAKING IN ARCHITECTURE ● ÖMER AKIN

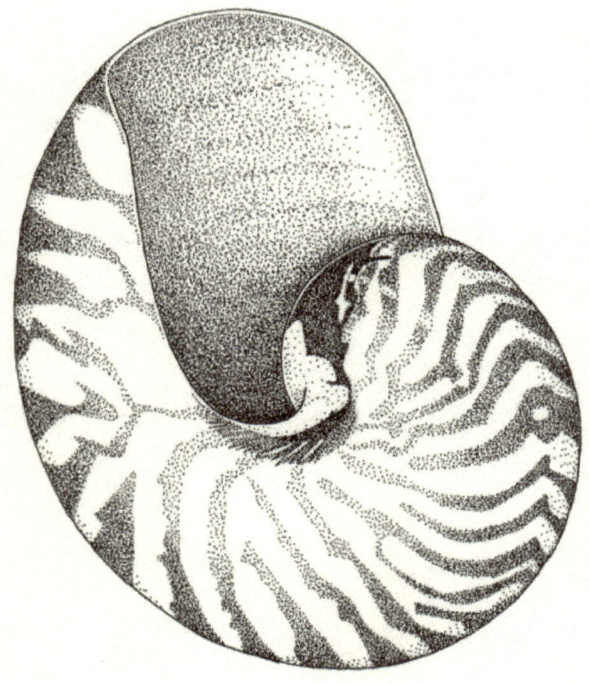

The Nautilus, based on the Fibonacci Series sketch by Ömer Akın

Chapter 14 Design Optimization

Optimization, the method *par excellence* in engineering fields, is conventionally used to determine the "best" solution among all possible available solutions. As opposed to the generative design methods where one develops new designs based on intuition and experience.

Optimization techniques are directed towards describing and selecting alternatives based on predefined criteria of selection. Hence, the emphasis is placed on *evaluation*, since the principal objective is to select one among all possible solutions that satisfies predetermined constraints. Since evaluation, as opposed to generation requires an altogether different "logic," and a different approach to design problems; representing optimization problems requires three key ingredients, *variables, constraints,* and *objective function(s)*.

Any problem that lends itself to this kind of formulation can be posed as an optimization problem. Under formal conditions,[xcvi] once such a problem description is obtained, standard techniques can be used to find the solution that will assign values to the variables so that the constraints are not violated and the objective function is satisfied. Since the parameters of the optimization problem can be mathematically defined, the evaluation of the optimization problem can be done quantitatively.[xcvii]

Architectural design problems are inherently difficult to formalize, in the mathematical sense, and to solve with optimization methods. In intuitive design, while solving problems, designers liberally define and redefine their problems.[xcviii]

In a problem domain like architecture, often called *ill-defined* (Reitman, 1964), constructing optimization problems is challenging. The possibility of optimizing ill-defined problems exists only when we observe certain restrictions. Radford and Gero (1986) define the following design optimization problem, articulating these restrictions:

Imagine an office block with continuous perimeter windows and a continuous horizontal sunshade above those windows... Imagine, too, that everything about the building is fixed except the height of the windows and projection of the sunshade. This gives us just two design variables to manipulate: we can combine different values of window height with different values of shade projection to yield tall, medium or short windows with extensive, medium or stubby shades...The windows cannot extend higher than the ceiling, and the sunshades are subject to a constructional constraint that restricts projection to a maximum of, say, 2 meters or so. These constraints together define a feasible region within which any design must lie.

In the authors' own words, this problem is rather "simple and artificial." This is due to the fact that there are many other variables relevant to the design problems, such as glazing type, depth of sill, functional requirements of a room, and lighting levels, which are difficult to formalize and control. Consider the formulation shown in Figure 25, under which the window design problem can be stated as an optimization problem. Here the solution should consist of a set of design values to be assigned to a set of design variables. If we were to assign a value for the height of the window, say h_w, and a value for the depth of the overhang, d_o, this could constitute a potential solution to the problem.

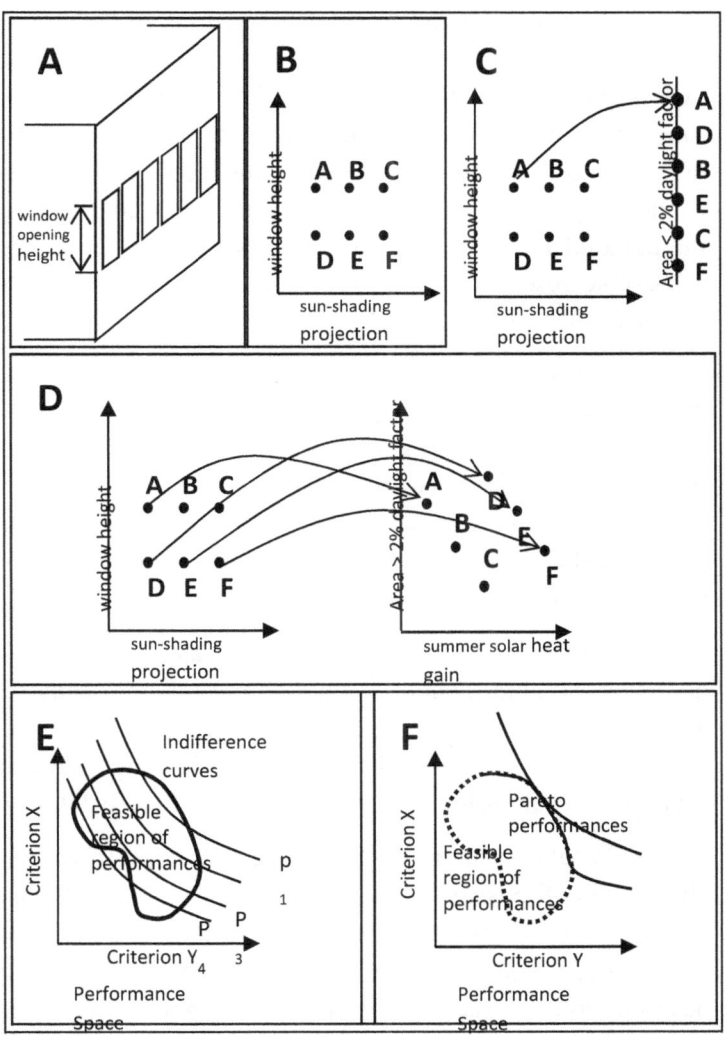

Figure 25: Window design as optimization (from Radford,1986)

For this to constitute a valid solution, these values, $V(h_w)$ and $V(d_o)$, would have to conform to the limitations set by the room height, facade orientation, and overhang cantilever dimensions. Furthermore, the performance expectations implied by it, in terms of room illumination and summer solar heat gain, would have to be within allowable ranges, specified by the objective function. Whether the client's objective is to maximize gain and/or to minimize illumination levels, the solution values must yield the best achievable result expected by the design variables and the objective function.

Let's dig a little deeper. Assume that we have six possible pairs of values for h_w and d_o: A, B, C, D, E, and F (Figure 25A). Let's also assume that the window heights for A, B, and C are the same and greater than those of D, E, and F, respectively. Furthermore, the sunshade projection for the pairs A and D, B and E, and C and F are the same, ordered in ascending fashion, respectively (Figure 25B).

Further, assume that the sunshade depth is the dominant variable. That is, it impacts most significantly the amount of daylight that penetrates the room. We can see this in the form of an ordinal vector showing daylight illumination values for A, D, B, E, C, and F (Figure 25C).

What is notable about such a graph is that if we were able to plot all possible value pairs for it, we would obtain a two-dimensional range which would mark the *"feasible performance region,"* or the range of all values that satisfy desirable solution states for the problem. Optimization of the problem, then, is the selection of the best solution among the entire set of alternatives, from all values in the feasible region.

In order to do this, tangible criteria are needed; criteria that will reflect the preferences of the designer and the client. The solution to the problem is shown in Figure 25 and contains the following steps:

o   Let us suppose that we are indifferent to a choice between a low heat gain and high daylight factor, say point A in Figure 25D, and a high heat gain and low daylight factor, say point F in the same figure.

o   Let us also suppose that we prefer moderate heat gain and daylight performance, either D or E, over either A or B. This suggests that we can represent our criteria of preference in the form of *isopreference* or *indifference curves* (Figure 25E).

The "best" solution, in this setting, would be represented by the point that is common to both the feasible region of performances and the highest valued indifference curve we can plot (Figure 25F).

To find this "best" solution, we took a graphic approach to the problem. While intuitively obvious and visually clear, such approaches do not easily scale up to optimization of full size building design problems. One reason for this is the inherent difficulty of searching within the graphic space, where a quantifiable, global metric indicating the likelihood of success in the search space, exists.

Another reason is the difficulty of specifying an objective function, such as, minimizing or maximizing one of the design values that can be represented graphically. Also there is no guarantee that there will not be better solutions that may not lend themselves to the graphic representation. Thus, the solution found may not necessarily be the best one but one that merely satisfies all of the stated constraints. Thus, more robust and accurate methods are necessary to determine and choose between potential solutions.

In the next example we introduce, we will consider two of these more robust methods: *Calculus* and the *Simplex* methods. In the Calculus method, the derivation of the optimal solution from the initial problem definition is carried out using methods of mathematical Differentiation.

This is a problem to find the optimal dimensions for the vaulted modules of L. I. Kahn's Kimbell Art Center in Texas. Let us add a few special constraints to make this optimization problem interesting. The mechanical system selected for the project dictates that the volume of each module should not exceed 20,000 cf. If this limit were to be exceeded, it would be better to move up to a system with greater capacity, in which case the maximum volume allocation for each module must be 30,000 cf.

The optimization task, then, is to determine the dimensions of the vaulted module so that its overall cost is minimized. Unit costs are given in Figure 26A. The complete formulation of this problem is shown in Figure 26B, which contains the following steps:

A Graphic representation of 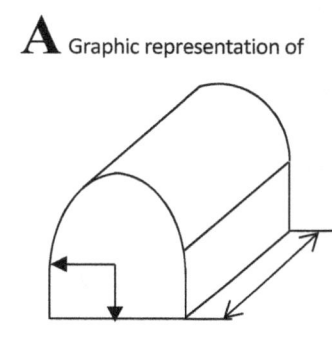	**B** Optimal Problem Formulation Roof area = πRL Endwall area = $0.5\pi R^2 + 2R^2$ = $(2 + 0.5\pi)R^2$ Volume = $(2 + 0.5\pi)R^2 L$ Cost = $15(\pi RL) + 60(2 + 0.5\pi)R^2$ = $15\pi RL + (120 + 30\pi)R^2$
Roof Cost = $15/sf Endwall Cost = $30/sf Sidewall Cost = $0/sf Volume = 20,000 cf Minimize Cost (objective function)	**C** Optimal Problem Solution $(2+0.5\pi)R^2 L = 20,000$ $L = 5,600/R^2$ $C = 47.12 R (5,600/R^2) + 214.24R^2$ = $214.24R^2 + 263,872/R$ $dC/dR = 428.48R + (263.872)R^{-2} = 0$ $428.48R^3 = 263.872$ $R = 8'6''; L = 77' 6'';$ $C = \$46,522.60$ Gallery width = 17'
D Design implications: The width of the space is too narrow (17") for a gallery space, therefore, let volume = 30,000 cf, and height = 2/3 R	
E Revised Problem Formulation Roof area = πRL Endwall area = $0.5\pi R^2 + 1.33R^2$ = $(1.33 + 0.5\pi)R^2$ Volume = $(2 + 0.5\pi)R^2 L$ Cost = $15(\pi RL) + 60(1.33 + 0.5\pi)R^2$ = $15\pi RL + (79.8 + 30\pi)R^2$	**F** Revised Problem Solution $(1.33+0.5\pi)R^2 L = 30,000$ $L = 10,330/R^2$ $C = 47.12R(10,330/R^2)+214.24R^2$ = $214.24R^2 + 486,760/R$ $dC/dR = 428.48R + (-86,760)R^{-2} = 0$ $428.48R^3 = 486,760$ $R^3 = 1,136; R = 10'5'';$ $L = 94' 11''; C = \$70,029$ Gallery width = 21'

Figure 26: Optimized solution for the vaulted space design problem

1. Find an expression for the areas of surfaces to be built.
2. Find an expression for the module's volume, based on 1.
3. Use 1 to find an expression for the module's cost.
4. Set volume equal to 20,000 cf. as required.
5. Find an expression equal to one of the variables, i.e., length of the module (L), in terms of the other, that is the radius of the vault (R).
6. Substitute expression from 5 into the expression in 3, reducing the number of unknowns.

This yields an expression that states the cost of the project in terms of one variable, namely the vault-radius. Since this is a quadratic function, differentiating this expression with respect to the radius and setting it equal to zero can yield the minimum or maximum points of this function (Figure 26B). Thus, we find that R = 8' 6", and L = 77' 6" (Figure 26C). This insures that the volume of the resulting design will not exceed 20,000 cf.; the section of the module will fit into a square and the cost of each module will be $46,522, which is the least cost under the constraints specified (Figure 26D).

This is a truly unique optimal solution that satisfies all of the stated constraints and minimizes costs as required by the objective function. Any other set of values for R and L will result in costs that exceed this requirement. Yet, it is quite conceivable that this may not be the preferred solution for a variety of reasons.

It is conceivable, for example, that the overall width of the module (17') would not be suitable for the exhibition function due to a number of problems like circulation, lighting, or size of exhibits.

At this point, the designer may want to alter some of the initial assumptions of the formulation. To illustrate the point, Figure 26D shows the way the problem can be reformulated:

1. By making the height to radius ratio 2:3, and
2. By moving to the next volumetric threshold: 30,000 cf.

Following the same steps followed earlier, Figure 26E and Figure 26F show the new problem formulation and solution, respectively. This yields an increase in the width the module to 21' achieving the desired effect of the reformulation.

Not all problems of optimization can be mapped into a graphic representation or the method of Calculus. Some problems involve so many variables that either method may become difficult or impossible to use. In these cases, where certain conditions are met; a technique called the Simplex Method can be used:

1. Variables are continuous and take values => than 0.
2. Constraints are a linear function of the variables.
3. Objective function is a linear function of variables.

The operations of the Simplex Method are in essence analogous to the graphical method. However, they are mapped into the numerical domain so that optimal solutions can be estimated using Matrix Algebra.

Design optimization is the closest that design Decision Making comes to the "rational" mode of decision making. In order for this optimization technique to be applicable, however, it must be possible not only to express the major design alternatives mathematically, but also to estimate the tradeoffs between them quantitatively. The burden of success of this approach then is more in formulating it than solving it. A successful formulation all but guarantees the best solution that there is, provided that there is at least one available.

Ethical Decision Making in Architecture
Part IV
Case Studies
Architectural-Engineering

Aristotele (384 BC – 322 BC)

Cover Image

Aristotele (384 BC – 322 BC)

The ancient Greek philosopher covered a wide range of subjects including biology, zoology, music, theatre, physics, politics, rhetoric, linguistics and morality. He made important contributions to just about all fields of knowledge that existed in his time. Along Socrates and Plato, Aristotle is one of the key figures in the emergence of Western philosophy and thought.

Part IV   Case Studies:
           Architectural-Engineering

Chapter 15   Citicorp Tower

Chapter 16   John Hancock Tower's

Chapter 17   K. C. Hyatt Regency Hotel

Figure 27 Citicorp Tower, Downtown, New York

Chapter 15 Citicorp Tower

The Citicorp Tower is a 59-story, mid-Manhattan tower well known for its unique urban form (Figure 27). It is supported by four nine-story columns located at the center points of its peripheral spans, rather than its four corners. This peculiarity is a result of the deal that Citicorp had to strike with the St. Peter's Church, which occupies one of the corners of the site (Figure 28), in order to purchase air rights from them.

It was this unique form that triggered a series of events, which eventually lead the principal design engineer of the building, William LeMessurier, to discover major structural design flaws. The discovery was surrounded by a certain drama highlighting important professional and ethical issues. Arguably, it was a matter of time, in fact possibly a matter of weeks, before a major calamity would be caused by the collapse of the building.

LeMessurier, the first and only person who discovered the structural flaws of the building, was under no legal obligation to reveal these problem, particularly not before, as his lawyers would argue, he was covered by more substantial professional liability insurance. Nevertheless, he went ahead with his disclosure and a series of remarkable events followed in solving the structural problem and averting grave danger to the building as well as surrounding properties.

Figure 28: St. Peter's Church on the Citicorp Plaza site, Downtown, New York

Figure 29 Tuned Mass Damper Casing, Citicorp Plaza, Downtown, New York

In 1977, when Citicorp Tower was completed, it was the 4th tallest structure in the world. Due to its support pillars, unique top, and several engineering innovations, its design was considered to be exceptional. Aside from the special location of the four pillars, the cross bracing concealed behind its slick, exterior cladding, and its super-light steel structure, it was also credited with one of the very early, successful applications of a *Tuned Mass Damper*. This mechanism, consisting of two 400-410 ton, free floating concrete blocks, was installed at the top floor of the tower in order to reduce the excessive sway of the tower due to lateral wind forces (Figure 29).

The structural pillars that carry the building go up the entire length of the 59-story, 914' high, building. The structure of the building is constructed entirely of steel. Six tiers of eight braces, forty-eight in all, clad the tower on all four sides thereby securing it against lateral wind loads. The frame of the building and the bracing to counteract lateral wind loads constitute 25,000 tons of steel. Compared to the 60,000 ton superstructure of the Empire State Building, Citicorp is considered super-light and inexpensive. This was the principal factor that helped keep the entire tower's cost to $175 million.

Early Findings

In June 1978, soon after the building's completion, a student from New Jersey called Mr. LeMessurier inquiring about the building's structural framing and safety in light of the unusual location of its supporting pillars. LeMessurier was confident of his design and explained to the student how the cross bracing helped lateral stability and reduced cost.

This innocent exchange lead to LeMessurier's decision to use this case as an example in a course he was teaching at the time and to re-calculate the strength of the entire structure particularly against lateral and quartering winds that applied to the design of this building due to its unusual geometry. While the quartering wind calculations would be relevant primarily because of this geometry they were not considered at the time of the initial design.

LeMessurier was surprised to find that the quartering winds calculations he did showed an increase in the design loads by %40 on the overall tower and %160 on at least half of the bracing elements. Yet, with the strong welded connections between the bracing and the building frame, plus the Tuned Mass Damper (Figure 29), the building was in no danger of failure.

Soon after, by mere coincidence, when LeMessurier was serving as a consultant for another tall structure in Pittsburgh, he discovered another structural problem, entirely unrelated to the first one. In this case, he was trying to persuade Bethlehem Steel, the steel manufacturer of the U.S. Steel Tower, to consider a bracing system similar to the one used at the Citicorp Tower.

At one point, he decided to call his office in New York to ascertain the connection details of the design for Citicorp. To his surprise, he learned that upon the request of Bethlehem Steel, the manufacturer for Citicorp at that time, the welded connection designs were substituted with bolted connections.

When this substitution was made, it appeared to be a reasonable decision since the safety factors used in design normally insure the structure's strength against the reductions that can occur in subsequent modification of its design. However, it was a revelation to him that his New York branch office had not informed him of the change. Now the safety of his design was challenged by two separate factors: quartering winds and bolted connections.

About a month following this discovery, LeMessurier decided to double-check all of the design calculations of the building. Unexpectedly, he discovered that not only were the quartering winds not taken into account, but the calculations were based on the assumption that the cross bracings of the building were to be considered trusses rather than columns. While this was permitted by American Institute of Steel Construction (AISC) standards, with the change to bolted connections, the joints were inadequate to withstand the tensile loads that would be produced in a 16-year storm.

LeMessurier faced a dilemma: to disclose or not to disclose these findings. If he did, his reputation and professional life as an engineer would be in jeopardy. If he did not, damage to many lives and property could occur. His lawyers were advising him to be cautious; while his wife and his personal instinct were pushing him in the direction of complete transparency.

Resolution

The solution to these problems turned out to be as unfathomable as the circumstances that brought them to light. Against legal advice and emboldened by Ms. LeMessurier support of his decision, Mr. LeMessurier revealed the facts he discovered to the representatives of the Citicorp brass, and their technical and legal consultants. Unexpectedly, he had a hard time convincing them that there was something wrong with their 1-year old headquarters building that received so much positive press.

After he succeeded in gaining the attention of the Citicorp officials, he had an equally hard time convincing them that there was nothing else wrong. In the month of June, which was upon them, strategies to save the building had to be developed:

1. Remedy the problem before the hurricane season hit.
2. Prevent public panic.
3. Figure out a way of fixing the bracing problem.
4. Find a way of paying for it all.

The hurricane season was indeed around the corner. In fact, during the repair period a hurricane heading towards New York fortunately turned around and went out into the Atlantic Ocean sparing the building and the crews who were feverishly working to repair its steel frame connections. The repair work was concealed by scheduling work during evening hours and placing workers inside wooden enclosures built around effected areas. The repair involved the welding of an H shaped "Band-Aid" where the giant cross braces met the building frame. This required the removal of all interior finishes and then their reinstallation before the repair task would move up to a higher floor.

To prepare for the worst-case scenarios, local officials and the Red Cross were mobilized to take census of nearby buildings' occupants and to prepare evacuation plans ready to go into effect in the event of an emergency. All parties were sensitive to the issue of concealing the gravity of the situation from the public in order to prevent panic.

LeMessurier's good fortune seemed to help him once again. Just as the press wised up to what was going on, New York papers went on strike for a duration that included the entire repair period, leaving the censure around the repair activity in tack. Also, the Tuned Mass Damper, which would help the structural integrity of the building during a storm, was equipped with an emergency generator.

When all was said and done, the estimated cost of the entire operation turned out to be around $4 million. Since much of the repair was done under emergency conditions, the real cost estimate was much higher. Also, not all expenditures were added to LeMessurier's debit column. Even with this optimistic bottom line, his insurance would cover only half of the $4M. estimate. In the end, Citicorp agreed to take care of the entire deficit.

LeMessurier's professionalism, forthrightness, and diligence had won many over to his side and he was spared the brunt of the actual costs. In the end, due to the fact that his actions averted a much larger potential claim, his insurance company decided to reduce his premiums.

Issues

This case study is an introduction to the Virtue Ethics framework as well as a Benefit-Cost coordination between different players of the professional office. Since LeMessurier has been hailed as the example of honesty, fairness, and integrity by many, Virtue Ethics is perfectly applicable to this case, while other ethics frameworks, such as Teleology, and Deontology, are also relevant.

The decision making method that comes to the fore is Risk-Cost-Benefit Analysis (Chapter 12). There were multiple tiers of communication between five levels, including: the boss in the main office, principals in charge of the local offices, project managers in charge of individual projects, designers responsible for specific aspects of each project, and draftsmen. Furthermore a project of this magnitude has several million parts that have to be assembled at the construction site.

A manager is faced with the prospect of assigning resources to tasks, in this case numerous communication tasks, while making sure that large portions of the budget are not spent just on communication and project planning (Chapter 13). This involved a myriad of protocols to be relayed to all members of the office and to a conglomeration of several offices. In particular, the lack of communication with LeMessurier about critical decisions like the bolted connections and the selection of a lower safety factor was a serious lapse. It's remarkable that it took chance events to reveal them, just in time to avert disaster.

ETHICAL DECISION MAKING IN ARCHITECTURE ● ÖMER AKIN

John Hancock Tower, Copley Square, Boston

Chapter 16 John Hancock Tower Is Falling

Robert Campbell, who has published a Pulitzer Prize winning expose on the triumphs and travails of the John Hancock Tower in Boston wrote the following memorable words: *"A high wind blew in Boston on the night of January 20, 1973."* On that fateful day, dozens of the 4.5' x 11.5' plate glass windows of the building cracked and sent dangerous shards onto the sidewalks below.

While the Hancock Tower has been one of the most celebrated buildings of the 70s, this was due to its failures as much as its successes. Arguably a masterpiece in terms of formal composition, its architects strove to realize many innovations and take some design risks in order to achieve its prominent place in the history of Modern Architecture. Eventually, it became a landmark among all the other landmarks of Copley Plaza.

Its many innovations include its unique massing, reflective skin (Figure 30), and the Tuned Mass Damper to keep it from swaying excessively. Yet these did not prevent the building's early years to be free from serious challenges. Some argued that this was the outcome of its innovations rather than their lack. The building worked its way through four major problems:

o Settlements causing damage to adjoining structures.
o Risk of excessive and structurally dangerous oscillations along the short direction of the building's footprint.
o Risk of toppling of the entire building in the long direction of its foot print.
o Breakage of the plate glass windows (Figure 31)..

The siting of the tower has been a difficulty from the very beginning. This has been a contributing factor to all of its early problems. At the same time, in terms of urban and historical appropriateness it has attracted considerable attention. In 1968, during a conference organized at the Boston Architectural Center expressly for reviewing the building's siting, it was hailed as an exemplary public and private collaboration. Eventually, all of these problems were resolved. Today, having received numerous design awards, the building stands as a distinguished neighbor of the Trinity Church, H. H. Richardson's masterpiece (Figure 30).

Resolution

In the early seventies, during the foundation stages of its construction, adjoining buildings including the Trinity Church and underground utility lines sustained structural damage due to excessive settlement caused by the tower's excavation cavity. The sheet piling and its lateral braces turned out to be inadequate. Engineers monitoring the rate of settlement in adjoining structures observed perfect correlation with the rate of excavation. This problem was resolved after installation of additional excavation bracing and repairs to the damaged structures.

The remaining three problems were not manifested until one of them, namely the plate glass breakage, started during the fateful windstorm of January 1973. Naturally, the attention of the engineers commissioned from the outset, as well as some retained subsequently, was focused on lateral resistance and motion related problems. Many diagnostic activities were undertaken based on extensive data gathered from the site using sensors and laboratory tests.

Figure 30: Reflection of Trinity Church on the glazed cladding of the John Hancock Tower, Boston

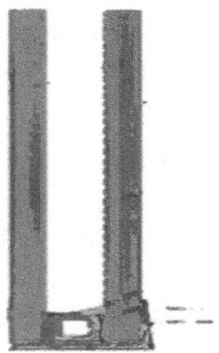

Figure 31: Plywood cladding replacing broken glass, John Hancock Tower

Figure 32: Double glazed cladding detail, John Hancock Tower

Eventually, Hanson, Holley and Biggs, a Boston firm, was hired to solve the glass breakage problem. At first, they decided to examine the building's frame and settlement conditions. Their initial discovery was unrelated to the breakage problem. The building tended to sway excessively in the wind, which they concluded, could be uncomfortable to the occupants. Since not very many modern towers were built before 1970, this was a state of the art issue. At the time, John Reed who was doing pioneering research at MIT on comfort conditions in high-rise towers was invited to join the team.

Eventually, it was decided that a Tuned Mass Damper system like the one designed by LeMessurier for the Citicorp Building in New York should be installed for the Hancock Tower. However, in wind tunnel tests, Mr. Hanson also found that the Tower was subject to excessive oscillation due to combined effects of lateral forces and torsional ones in the short direction of the building's footprint. Two international experts, one on steel structures, Bruno Thurliman, and the other on wind tunnel testing, A. G. Davenport, were added to the team.

After more testing, yet another unexpected problem emerged as a principal concern. Thurliman concluded that the structure was well braced in the short direction but was vulnerable in the long direction due to the weakness of braces and the second order effect of gravity loads due to lateral deflection. This problem could be resolved by strengthening the bracing of the frame in the long direction, which was done. However, in spite of all of this, the glass breakage problem remained unresolved.

Eventually, the cause of the glass breakage problem was discovered through the method of elimination. Once the structural frame and motion problems were fixed, as the potential causes of the breakage problem, attention was focused on the cladding system. A group of experts, including engineers William LeMessurier and Victor Mahler, began to study the problem through monitoring of the site conditions, wind tunnel experiments, and the construction of the cladding panel itself.

Their conclusions pointed to the unusual and unexpected bonding that formed between the lead spacer separating the two panes of glass and the reflective silver coating applied to the inner surface of the outer glass pane (Figure 32). Because of this bonding, the lead spacer and the outer glass pane were behaving as if they were a monolithic material. This resulted in the lead spacer developing fatigue since the flexing of the pane of glass due to wind velocity was transferred directly to the lead spacer.

While glass could withstand the flexing, material properties of lead were different and fatigue developed rapidly. Once this happened, cracks began to form in the lead. Subsequently, these "weak" spots started causing differential bending in the glass. Eventually the glass also started showing fatigue at these points and small cracks appeared. Subject to the continuous and variable wind loads these cracks began to telegraph throughout the entire pane ultimately resulting in shards of glass separating from the cladding and falling onto the pavements. This was accelerated during strong winds, causing dozens of panes to break in the span of a short period of time.

The reason why this problem was not easily discovered, or that no one was able to anticipate it, is largely due to the fact that this was one of the very few times the specific materials of cladding assembly were used together, especially the silver coating and the soldered lead spacer. Once the problem was identified, the solution was clear and quite costly. All 10,344 glazed cladding panels were replaced with a similar assembly excluding the lethal combination of spacing materials as well as the double glazing that served to reduce UV penetration.

Groups of experts who examined this issue and finally solved the problem were working under an agreement of non-disclosure, in perpetuity. The only two individuals who, perhaps by some fortunate oversight, had not signed this agreement were LeMessurier and Mahler. Twenty years later, they disclosed the mysterious circumstance of Hancock Tower's falling glass, entirely on their own volition.

Critical Issues

Decision Making Methods of Interest

Innovation in design is not a guarantee for success. In order to succeed, some innovations require true genius in management, finance, planning, and design, such as in the case of the Crystal Palace, (Chapter 8). Others succeed at the expense of budget and schedule limits. like the Sydney Opera House (Chapter 5) and Fallingwater (Chapters 7). Yet others, Pruitt-Igoe (Chapter 9), K.C. Hyatt Regency (Chapter 17), experience failure; or John Hancock Tower (current Chapter 16) and Citicorp Tower (Chapter 15) with near failure.

The rhetorical question is; what accounts for these differences? An easy to say but difficult to prove answer is: innovative design features must be tested with full and complete modeling prior to their all-out installation. This has been demonstrated in the case of both successes and failures that we reviewed. Time and budget pressures and difficult to integrate communication protocols between construction managers, engineers, and designers, are often the primary reasons for falling prey to these shortcomings.

Relevant Applied Ethics Frameworks

Ethics of Relativity, applicable in the Hancock case, is easily misunderstood. It is many things but none of them include "anything goes." It simply is a counterpoint to "absolutism." This is almost tautological; there is no moral imperative that holds for all people, places, times, and cultures.

By the same token, there is always a compelling moral imperative given a specific person, time, location or culture. We can deduce in hindsight that, in some cases, the economic and urban design urgencies, blind-sighted the decision makers to envision projects far more ambitious than they had to be.

In contrast, Virtue Ethics embodies a tenet based on human character. In the Hancock case there were heroes like Thurliman, Davenport, Mahler, and LeMessurier who rose above the occasion. Yet, Virtue Ethics is relevant only to specific cultures and times, such as for Aristotle in Ancient Greece.

ETHICAL DECISION MAKING IN ARCHITECTURE ● ÖMER AKIN

Functions Lobby of the K.C. Hyatt Regency After the collapse, Kansas City, Missouri

Chapter 17 K.C. Hyatt Regency Hotel

On July 17, 1981, two suspended walkways within the atrium area of the Hyatt Regency Hotel in Kansas City, MO, collapsed, leaving 113 people dead and 186 injured. In terms of loss of life and injuries, this was the most devastating structural collapse ever to take place in the United States.[xcix]

The Investigation

On July 17, 1981, Senator Thomas F. Eagleton's office contacted the National Bureau of Standards and requested that technical assistance be provided to Kansas City. Shortly thereafter Kansas City Mayor, Richard L. Berkley asked National Bureau of Standards (NBS) to determine the most probable cause of the walkways' collapse. Senators Thomas F. Eagleton and John C. Danforth and Congressman Richard Bolling endorsed the Mayor's request for this independent investigation.

NBS researchers first arrived in Kansas City on July 21, 1981. After extensive laboratory tests and onsite inspections NBS issued a report summarizing its findings. During the course of the investigation, the NBS team of engineers and scientists inspected the Hyatt Regency atrium area and the warehouse where the walkway debris was stored. They concluded that the walkways that collapsed were designed and constructed in a substandard manner directly contributing to the collapse. No other factor was linked to the disaster.[c]

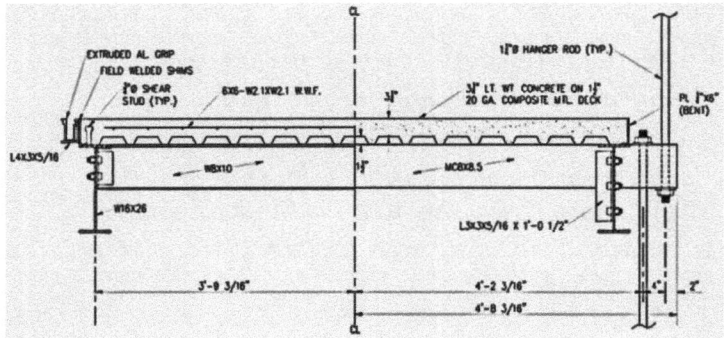

Figure 33: Cross section of walkways, Kansas City, Missouri[ci]

In the early phases of the investigation, NBS's involvement was limited by court order to visual observations and measurements. NBS requested permission to weigh selected walkway spans and to remove for additional study and destructive examination certain portions of the walkway box beams, hanger rods, concrete decks, and nuts and bolts.

Documents such as drawings, specifications, inspection reports, test reports, and construction logs, as well as photographs and videotapes became available to NBS from a number of sources. These were useful in gaining information about the walkways as originally approved for construction and as modified during the construction process.[cii] NBS conducted extensive laboratory tests on fabricated mockups of parts of the walkways, and on portions of the debris. Analytical models were developed to predict the response of the walkways to various loading conditions. Also, tests were conducted to determine material properties and weld and fracture characteristics.

The Design

The Hyatt Regency consists of three main sections: a high-rise section, a function block, and a connecting atrium area. Three suspended walkways spanned the atrium at the second third and fourth floor levels and connected the high-rise block to the function floors.

The second floor walkways were suspended from the fourth floor walkway, which was directly above it. In turn, this fourth floor walkway was suspended from the atrium roof held up by a set of six hanger rods. The third floor walkway was offset from the other two and was independently suspended from the roof framing by another set of hanger rods.[ciii]

In the collapse, the second and fourth walkways fell to the atrium floor, with the fourth floor walkway coming to rest on the lower walkway. Most of those killed and injured were either on the first floor level of the atrium or on the second floor walkway. The third floor walkway was not involved in the collapse.[civ]

The Hanger Rods

As originally approved by the Kansas City Codes Administration Office, the plans for the walkways called for a single set of hanger rods to be attached to the roof framing. These rods have had to pass through the fourth floor box beams and on through to the second floor box beams. The box beams – made up of a pair of 8-inch steel channels with the flanges welded toe to toe – were to rest on hanger-rod washers and nuts below each set of beams.

Under this arrangement each box beam would separately transfer its load directly onto the hanger rods.[cv] However, during construction, shop drawings were prepared by the steel fabricator, which called for the use of two sets of hanger rods rather than a single set. Based on the original design the entire second floor walkway load was first transferred to the fourth floor box beams, where both that load and the fourth floor walkway loads were transmitted through the box beam-hanger rod connections to the ceiling hanger rods (Figure 33).

As indicated by their stamps, the contractor, structural engineer, and architect acknowledged reviewing the shop drawings.[cvi]

Efforts were made to establish as accurately as possible the loads on the walkways at the time of the collapse. Weighing of selected walkway debris along with measurements taken on concrete cores removed from the walkway decks permitted NBS to determine that the actual walkway dead load was approximately 8% higher than the nominal dead load, which is an estimate based solely on the project's contract drawings.[cvii]

Estimates of the live loads due to people present on the walkways at the time of the collapse were much more difficult to make. Witnesses made a number of conflicting statements regarding the numbers of people on the walkways just prior to the collapse. A television crew had videotaped parts of the walkway minutes before the collapse. By studying this videotape, NBS concluded that 63 people were on the second and fourth floor walkways at the time of collapse, which did not exceed design live load estimates.[cviii]

Findings

Based on field, laboratory and analytical investigations, NBS concluded that:[cix]

1. Collapse of the walkways occurred under the action of loads that were substantially less than the design loads specified by the Kansas City Building Code.
2. The ultimate capacity of box-beam hanger rod connections could be predicted on the basis of laboratory test results.
3. Under the action of the loads estimated to have been present on the walkways at the time of collapse, all fourth floor box-beam hanger rod connections were candidates for the walkway to collapse.
4. Observed distortions of structural components strongly suggested that failure of the walkway system initiated in the box beam-hanger rod connections at location 9UE (east end of middle box beam on the fourth floor).
5. As constructed, the box beam-hanger rod connections, the fourth floor to ceiling hanger rods, and the third floor walkway hanger rods did not satisfy the design provisions of the Kansas City Building Code.
6. The change in the hanger rod arrangement from a continuous rod to interrupted rods doubled the load to be transferred by the fourth floor hanger-rod connections.
7. The box beam-hanger rod connections would not have satisfied the Kansas City Building Code under the original hanger rod detail (continuous rod).
8. Under the original hanger rod arrangement (continuous rod) the box beam-hanger rod connections as shown on the contract drawings would have had the capacity to resist the loads estimated for the time of collapse.

9. Neither the quality of workmanship nor the materials used in the walkway system played a significant role in initiating the collapse.

Critical Issues

Decision Making Method Employed

Crisis management through *Integrated Design Delivery* and *Interoperability* protocols are two of the most challenging advances in building design fields. Without better coordination between delivery stages, loss of time, accuracy and increased risk of catastrophic failure were expected. Remedies would include product modeling, Integrated Design Delivery, and introduction of new regulations.

In this case the change of design approval process was flawed. Even though the modified design meant doubling of the loads on the washers of the 4th floor box beam connections the architects, engineers and contractors did not sufficiently scrutinize this design.

Relevant Applied Ethics Framework

Teleology is the gold standard of ethics in professional practice particularly when harm to property and life are involved. It is directly related to the concept of a collective assessment for a multitude of diverse stakeholders, which is the prevailing state of affairs in the office: including consultants, financiers, contractors, clients, and engineers.

The K.C. Hyatt case needs no elaborate analysis to observe the result of mistakes in the design modification processes which led to the number of dead, injured and property damage. In this case, the greater good suffered more than in any other case that we studied.

Ethical Decision Making in Architecture — Ömer Akin

Ethical Decision Making in Architecture

Part V
Epilogue: *Applied Ethics Anecdotes*

Renatus Cartesius (1596–1650)

Cover Image

Renatus Cartesius (René Descartes; 1596–1650)

He was a French philosopher, mathematician, and scientist. Dubbed the father of modern western philosophy, much of subsequent Western philosophy is a response to his writings, which are studied closely to this day.

Part V   Applied Ethics Anecdotes

Preface   What is Applied Ethics?
Episode 1   Air in Mainland China
Episode 2   Technology and Mental Health
Episode 3   What's with Industrial Farming?
Episode 4   Water, the Next Global Crisis
Episode 5   Funding Our Climate
Episode 6   A Tale of Revenge Gone Wrong
Episode 7   Lawyer Purchases a Box of Cigars

Preface: What is Applied Ethics?

Doing our best as professionals to dispense of our responsibilities and to aid our profession along with our careers does not necessarily mean that by doing so we automatically become ethical. Maintaining the integrity of our design ideas, in the end, may be irrelevant if, for instance, our design, however brilliant, is an extermination camp for the efficient processing of inmates.

Similarly, doing our best by sticking to the most popular or objective reasoning in making choices about good design, as members of the administration or faculty of a school of architecture, does not necessarily mean that we have been fair or virtuous in meeting our moral responsibilities. It may be evident to the reader that the difficulty in sorting out these conflicts lies in the challenges of agreeing upon a commonly held set of theories, principles, or frameworks that can help us differentiate the moral from the immoral, set priorities between conflicting interests, and insure that the participation in these principles are free-willed.

Moral philosophers have traditionally aspired to normative theories of what is right or wrong. But, in applied ethics, a practical price is paid for generality. It is often unclear whether and if theories should be applied only in specific contexts and to particular cases.

Philosophers interested in applying their training to such problems share a conviction with persons from numerous other fields that decision making in these areas is fundamentally moral and of the highest social importance. The work of these philosophers in *Applied Ethics* often deals with realistic cases and actors. This means taking real or hypothetical cases and analyzing them to decide which course of action is the moral high road based on formal theories of morality. This method is called *Ethical Adjudication*.

In this Part of this text we will illustrate Ethical Adjudication through examples we call Episodes.[cx] Thus, a few cautions are in order. Many of the anecdotes in this book used as Applied Ethics material involve roles based on characters from annals of Philosophy as well as everyday life, all acted out by imaginary actors. These actors are referenced with an assigned "nickname" that resembles the name of the person whom they are imitating.

For example: Aristotele's imitator is called *Aristo*: J.S. Mill's imitator is called *Mill*; and Immanuel Kant's imitator is called *Kant*, and so on (*see next page*).

Table of Nicknames Actors and Roles		
Nicknames	Role Models	Real or Fictitious Roles
Alexander	Alexander the Great	Macedonian king, conqueror and student of Aristotele
Architect FLW	Frank Lloyd Wright	Famous American architect who had worldwide notoriety
Architect LC	Le Corbusier	Famous French architect who had worldwide influence
Architect LS	Louis Sullivan	Famous American architect who ushered in Modernism and mentored FLW
Architect MC	Marie Coyote	Architect who destroyed all office documentation
Aristo	Aristotele	(384 – 322 B.C.) Greek philosopher, student of Plato
Cicero	Cicero	(106-43 B.C.) He moved Greek philosophy, rhetoric into Latin
Confucius	Confucius	Universally known Chinese philosopher
Descartes	René Descartes	Renatus Cartesius (1596-1650} father of modern philosophy
Julian	Barbadian Butler	Who went mad and burned down FLW's office and killed inhabitants
Kant	Immanuel Kant	German philosopher central in modern philosophy
LaoTzŭ	LaoTzŭ	Elusive philosopher and founder of Taoism
Mencius	Mencius	Chinese Philosopher promoting ethics of benevolence
Mill	J. S. Mill	British Philosopher and Utilitarian ethicist
Ockham	William of Ockham	A fourteenth-century English philosopher
Plato	Plato	An ancient Greek philosophe and Aristotle's mentor
Rawls	John Rawls	Moral and political philosopher in the liberal tradition
Rumi	Mevlana Celaleddin-i Rumi	13th century Muslim saint and Anatolian mystic

Episode 1 Air in Mainland China[cxi]

Air in China

China's heavy pollution has been well documented for decades now. In 2015, Beijing issued two Red-Alerts for pollution, the highest level warning which calls for emergency measures such as closing schools and restricting car use. More recently, poor air quality is also having a significant effect on the tourist trade.

Some businesses are taking advantage of the air pollution problem. Providing food delivery services that meet the needs of those staying indoors; bars which push their air purifiers as a marketing tool to get customers; and beer that gets cheaper as the air quality gets worst.

Obviously these are neither long-term solutions nor beneficial ones to human health and wellbeing. According to Ma Jun,[cxii] one of China's most prominent environmentalists, "*China has reached its tipping point. It's time to change and look for good trade-offs between environmental quality and economic growth. If we don't do that, we're going to suffer a hard landing one day, very soon.*"

Engineering solutions from providing wind turbines and solar panels to NGOs and citizens forcing local government and industry to act, China's next steps are going to be closely scrutinized.

LaoTzŭ: "These doomsayers should be stopped by any means before they spoil the state of *wu wei*[cxiii] and intimidate the conduct of sound government. We need to embrace these new strategies of merchandize delivery, air purifiers and cheap beer. They are not short term solutions; they will help tide us over to more permanent solutions like finding the right trade-offs between growth and quality."

Mencius: "Humans are inherently benevolent. We have to trust that all will be well with just instincts."

Confucius: "But this is how we got to where we are today. *Kant* thinks it is not the rightness or wrongness of actions; it is the rightness or wrongness of the consequences of those actions or the character of the actor."

Mencius: "Why should we question the good deeds that individuals, even governments, are engaged in. The land is covered with wind turbines and solar panels anyway."

Confucius: "We cannot shirk our responsibilities. We have to be proactive, down to the last individual. This is an enormous problem. It can only be solved by considering all possible consequences and seek out the greater good. I believe *Mill* is more right than *Kant*."

LaoTzŭ: "I think we are more right than all of the Western philosophers put together. Let's trust our innate character and the direction we are heading: 'If you do not change direction, you may end up where you are heading.'"

Confucius: "Where we are heading is the demise of thousands due to lung and heart disease. Fatalistic thinking got us into many calamities before; it will do it again. While we pray for good Emperors, we endure whomsoever we end up with. This is because we trust that our own values will overcome what fate brings."

Mencius: "While we are waiting, pollution will take many citizens to their graves. Do we have the right to sacrifice them while we feel content with home delivery, cheap beer, and air purifiers? Don't we have the responsibility to interfere before it is too late?"

LaoTzŭ: "Do you have the patience to wait until your mud settles and the water is clear?"

Kant, Aristo, Mill, Rawls, Descartes, Confucius, Mencius and LaoTzŭ exchange high-fives and chant:

"Give up anger. Give up pride,
Free yourself from worldly bondage.
No sorrow can befall those who never try to possess others and things as their own."

Episode 2 Technology and Mental Health [cxiv]

Ellie and a Mental Health Patient

Ellie is a virtual interviewer, a machine that has been developed to help diagnose depression and post-traumatic stress disorder. Ellie is an example of the ways that technology can be put to good use by helping improve people's mental wellbeing. Clinical researchers say that contrary to common belief, technology can be a real safety net rather than a detriment to our mental health.

Given worldwide harm caused by depression, we have to embrace the development and adoption of new technologies. If we do not fall victim to the paranoia surrounding technology, such as the presumed damage that can be caused by microwave emissions from cellphones, we may realize breakthroughs that will accelerate medical cures to intractable ailments like dementia.

Kant: "It is disgraceful that anyone can contemplate sitting on their hands while people are falling off like flies; and what for? So the fat cats will continue to get fatter and government agents on the take will continue to appease the public with a false confidence in technology rather than initiating robust research about the human mind.

Everyone should read the "Critique of Pure Reason"[cxv] to understand what we already know about the human mind. I hate to toot my own horn but not everything under the sun is new."

Ockham: "Sure; but this is in too many words!"

Cicero: "If I remember my reading of *Kant's* "Critique" he pretty much attempted to explain the relationship between reason and human experience and to move beyond the failures of traditional philosophy or metaphysics. This may be good philosophy but how does it address the mental health issue? There is a lot more to figuring out why reason and human experience do not see eye to eye. While symptoms of dementia can vary greatly, at least two of the following five core mental functions must be impaired: memory, communication, ability to focus, reasoning, and judgment."

Ockham: "Why did Cicero steal away from the Senate under the dark of night?"

Oedipus: "Mental disorders are often misunderstood. While the status of overall mental healthcare is poor, people shy away from seeking help for their mental illnesses due to prevailing misconceptions, stigmas, and fears. Even *Sigmund* got it wrong when he stole a literary license from Shakespeare and made me the scapegoat. As a result some of the most heinous mental conditions are attributed to *"Oedipus Rex."*

Ockham: "You are mere fiction."

Mill: "Let us look at the winners and losers of each case. Do we harm more people by using the traditional medical techniques or by using this newfangled tool called *Ellie*? We do not know what kind of potential good and harm Ellie is likely to cause. If we did we could compare it to the reciprocal values of current practice. In this way we can maximize the overall good we can achieve in each case."

Rawls: "Yes but do we have the right to subject patients to these new procedures that are not proven to be safe and shown to improve treatment protocols? Is this Just? There cannot be morality without Justice."

Descartes: "*W*e should start from a clean slate. What makes us think that our predecessors were right? To make the world better we cannot be slowed down by taking an account of all harms that can be committed. We have to act rationally and pursue our responsibilities."

Ockham: "Just follow that which is right"

Sigmund: "The greatest question that has never been answered is: 'what does a woman like Ellie want?'"

Oedipus, Mill, Rawls, Descartes, Cicero, Ockham, chant in unison:

"Chauvinist!"
"Boooooooo!" "Boooooooo!" "Boooooooo!"
"Chauvinist!"

Episode 3 What's with Industrial Farming?[cxvi]

Factory Farm

Industrial farming methods are increasingly coming under criticism for the abundant use of antibiotics (more than 70% of the antibiotics sold in the US). Our growing resistance to antibiotics is caused by irresponsible practices of writing too many prescriptions; liberal use of medicines by patients; and uncontrolled use of medicines in farming for reasons other than legitimate disease prevention.

Antibiotics are used on industrial farms, in perfectly healthy animals, principally to promote growth of livestock or as a safeguard against routine diseases. These practices are the principal cause of antibiotic resistance in humans.

"As a recent Guardian editorial points out, 'Antibiotic resistance may not seem as urgent as terrorism or the NHS funding shortfall. But it is actually a threat that could kill many more people and degrade the quality of civilized life.' The Guardian's investigation into the poultry industry, a key user of antibiotics, has uncovered a catalogue of other disturbing practices. From alleged hygiene failings leading to contaminated chicken to serious concerns about working conditions. These revelations show the heavy price some pay for cheap chicken.

Then there's pesticide use. Numerous studies have suggested its links with a range of health impacts, including cancers and Parkinson's disease.

The French wine industry, where only 8.4% of vineyards are organic is one sector particularly enamored with pesticides. However, experts predict that dozens of legal proceedings could be in the pipeline across France related to their health impacts."

Mill: "Let us look at the winners and losers of each action. Do we harm more people by liberally using antibiotics when they are not needed or when they are used to stimulate animal growth? We do know what kind of potential harm excessive antibiotic use causes: proliferation of bacteria resistant germs, premature puberty, prolonged and expensive treatments of diseases, even death."

Rawls: "There is little to debate about the harm. The question is: what are the benefits of using antibiotics in the farm? The answer is: more and cheaper meats and other animal products resulting in greater profit for the farmers and longevity to farm animals. All of this is at the expense of human patients. The trouble is, farmers decide what happens solely based on their own interest and wellbeing. Who gave them the right to jeopardize human health and safety?"

Descartes: "Farmers have every right to decide for themselves; and look after their own interests. Do consumers have to buy the antibiotic laden meats? It's their freewill that is really in question. If they chose to eat contaminated meat who are we to stop them?"

Cicero: "What about common sense? Is there no advocate for commonsense to balance the interests of consumers against that of animal farmers? There are very few advocates taking up such causes."

Ockham: "Don't forget the government?"

Kant: "Governments are just place holders for our good will. Nothing is good without qualification except a good will, and a good will is one that wills to act in accord with moral law and out of respect for that law rather than inclinations."

Aristo: "It's a matter of integrity. Without the proper human character, principles will go only so far."

Confucius, LaoTzŭ, and Mencius begin chanting:

"Without human character, principles go only so far;

"Without human character, principles go only far;

"Without human character, principles go far.

Episode 4 Water: the Next Global Crisis[cxvii]

Polluted Stream

Globally, we now drink as much packaged water as we do milk, which is quite remarkable in two respects – the increase of the need for packaged water and the resurgence of milk consumption exceeding that of water. The human metabolism is not equipped to absorb lactose after the age of two; thus we should not be drinking any milk at all. However, we have trained ourselves to do so and most metabolisms have adapted to digesting milk with little if any problems, at all.

With this caveat, it seems that we have also transformed our water sources into an "unnatural" pattern of consumption by importing so much of it. For instance, despite the country having abundant sources of water, over one fifth of the water in the UK is sourced from overseas.

There have also been preferences for water from remote areas, such as Fiji Water, which is quite popular in the US and is sourced from the Fiji Islands, 1,600 miles from the nearest continent. In the context of a world that is struggling with acute water scarcity in many areas, there are serious questions to be answered about our role as the stewards of Earth.

Ockham: "I rest my case."

Oedipus: "What case? The narrative above is just a prologue to what is to follow. Even Shakespeare wrote in *The Tempest*, Act 2, Scene I: "What's past is prologue;" suggesting that all that has happened before that point in time, the 'past,' leads the characters to an opportunity to do what they are about to do."

Mill: "*Oedipus:* when did you cease to be a character in a play and become an interpreter of the playwright's intentions? You are reciting gibberish that has nothing to do with ethics. Can we cut the crap and look at the consequences. The problem of water will not be solved by moving bottled water on trucks, planes or on horseback. The *Utilitarian* will tell you that one's effort is better spent by conserving, distilling and collaborating with your neighbors to use it wisely. That is how we can enhance the greater good."

Confucius: "Virtue is more to man than either water or fire. I have seen men die from treading on water and fire, but I have never seen a man die from treading on the course of virtue."

Ockham: "Well put."

Rawls: "Inspiring but, virtuous or not, without a Just partitioning of the world's resources we will all perish. We have to support ethics with Justice."

Kant: "First, we have to recognize that world's resources belong to all of us; not more to those with more wealth or more power. If we trample on other's rights just because we can, we violate *Deontology,* the first principle of ethics."

Descartes: "I never thought I would say this about a fellow philosopher but *Kant* is right. It's our responsibility to make sure that all rights must be treated *justly.*"

Aristo: "I can't believe that the virtuous character has been tossed aside in favor of consequences and responsibilities. I understand if there is some fair calculation of the greater good, but to leave it up to others to recognize one's character – call it rights or whatever else you like – is false. Character is the foundation of virtue."

Ockham: "Silence is golden."

Aristo, Mencius, Cicero, LaoTzŭ, singing in the barbershop quartet style:
"Talking is cheap, people follow like sheep;
Even though, there is nowhere to go;
Silence is golden, but my eyes still see.

Episode 5 Funding Our Climate[cxviii]

Fixing the Climate is Very Expensive

Climate change is funded in numerous, often opaque ways, from the issuing of bonds that support the relentless expansion of palm-oil plantations to the lobby groups seeking to undermine government action on climate change.

Some argue that climate change leaders should join forces with fossil fuel companies to put a price on carbon. It has been documented that fossil fuel companies receive $5.3tn in worldwide subsidies every year – that's $10m a minute – exceeding global spending on every other sector including health. Pricing carbon fuels to reflect their true social and environmental impacts can help to speed up the transition to renewable energy and more energy efficient living standards.

Other ways to tackle climate change that have risen to prominence over the past year include scaling up the divestment movement and driving more investment into renewables. The divestment campaign has had some recent successes, including Californian law makers passing a bill to require the state's two largest pension funds to divest from coal. Several multi-billion-dollar high-tech companies are working on creating coalitions to support early-stage clean energy.

Oedipus: "I never knew before I came to the States that Shakespeare was into oil and gas. The *Shakespeare Oil Company, Inc.* is a family owned, independent company engaging in drilling, exploration and purchase of oil and gas properties. It currently operates over 320 active oil and gas wells in Illinois, Indiana, Kansas,

Montana, Oklahoma and Wyoming. William would be proud to see his name in neon lights on a marquis."

Ockham: "More dribble."

Confucius: "Ockham you expressed an idea in more than ten characters. *Zhège Suōláihuàcháng* – meaning: there's a lot more to say about that."

Mill: "This is huge. If you get big tech companies with big bucks to support early-stage clean energy that can get the coalition of individuals and governments to work towards 'Ethics with Justice;' we can avoid abandoning individual interests, rights, and create a path towards reaching the greater good."

Rawls: "I do not want to beat up on a dead horse but virtues are only relevant in the context of a strong framework, like *Justice Ethics*. How can two adversaries like climate change leaders and fossil fuel companies join forces; or how can we achieve issuing of bonds to lobbyists without a Just basis?"

Aristo: "What role does virtue play in all of this? Do you think *Teleology* and *Deontology* are achievable without a sound doze of character? Could climate-change-leaders join forces with fossil fuel companies without an abundance of *courage*? Doesn't the issuing of bonds to lobby groups require an unusual kind of *temperance*?

And without a foundation of *liberality* won't the dream of putting a price on carbon die a long painful death?"

Descartes: "We are dancing at the fringes of the problem. Rights and responsibilities are the only forces powerful enough to deal with such an enormous problem. It is not just individuals and governments we are talking about; it is the well-being of the entire globe that is at risk."

Kant: I will return the favor, which was payed to me earlier by my French colleague. We have to trust *Deon* and the good sense of the populous, in order to hold in high esteem that which we want to see given to them."

Ockham: "More garbage."

Mencius: "Only two words. I'll take it!"

Cicero: "I have lawyered and judged a lot of tricky cases. I think rights and responsibilities have it."

An anonymous group of Taoist monks chanting:
"Rights and Responsibilities,
Responsibilities and Rights,
Rights and Rights,
Rights and More Rights…
and Responsibilities."

Rumi

"Raise your words, not your voice. It is rain that grows flowers, not thunder."

Episode 6 A Tale of Revenge Gone Wrong

Architect MC

When *Architect MC*– a pseudonym to protect the innocent – of Florida saw a help-wanted ad in the newspaper for a position that looked suspiciously like her current job; and with her boss' phone number listed, she assumed she was about to be fired. The following Sunday night, late, she went to the office where she works and erased several years-worth of electronic drawings and blueprints, estimated to be worth $4.3 million.

"She decided to mess up everything for everybody," the Sheriff's Office spokesman told reporters. "She just sabotaged the entire business, thinking she was going to get axed." A mug shot of *Architect MC* was released by the Gainesville Sheriff's Office.

It didn't take Holly Hawking, the owner of the architectural firm that bears her name, much time to figure out "who'd done it." *Architect MC* was the only other person who had full access to the files. Police arrested her Sunday evening and charged her with causing greater than $5,000 damage to computer files: a felony. She was bailed out the following afternoon. Holly Hawking told one TV station that she'd managed to recover all of the files using an expensive data-recovery service.

As for the job, *Architect MC* wasn't in danger of losing it. The ad was for Holly Hawking's husband's company. The firm told CAYOTENews.com that "*Architect MC* is no longer employed here."

Architect FLW: "When I used to work for *Architect LS* we kept all drawings in locked flat-files. Being his right-hand boy, I was the keeper of the keys, besides *Architect LS*, that is. If some calamity befell the files, that would be the end of me. Everyone knew this and made sure I was aware of their comings and goings. At my Arizona office, one of my employees kept everyone honest. That is a form of ethical behavior isn't it?"

Architect LC: "There was one intern who kept loitering around the flat-file area. He knew I was onto him, it turns out he was trying to impress me. Poor boy, he had his hormones all mixed up."

Architect FLW: "But if he had done something like the *Architect MC* or heaven forbid like Julian, my former servant at my Eastern branch office, over the fear of being fired, he would have been toast. Don't these people have any regard for other's rights? What about their responsibilities to safeguard art, architecture, and property, not to mention human life. *Architect MC*'s misdeeds pale in comparison to those of Julian, who set fire to the building and slaughtering eight innocents."

Architect LC: "*FLW* you are applying your ethical norms to unfortunate lackeys, a confused underling and a deranged servant from Barbados. They were selfish and when it came to their own interests they behaved like judge, jury and executioner. They had very little regard for the rights of others."

Kant: "You have to look at it from their standpoint too: the big bad boss-man's responsibilities and the rights of the entire office should not override individual rights."

Architect LC: "It is okay to *infringe* on the rights of the individual so long as you do not *violate* them; however the tables are turned here. Where do these employees find the *chutzpah* – a term I learned from a Jewish client – to violate the rights of the entire office?"

Architect LS: "If these people were unfairly fired – I know, *I know*, that was not the case – but say that they were; then would their actions be justified?"

Mill: "Not even then; where would we be if any disgruntled employee took the law into their hands?"

Architect LC, Architect FLW, Architect LS, Architect MC, Kant, and J.S. Mill chanting in unison:

"Rights and Responsibilities run supreme; Wrights and W-responsibilities run amok; Wrongs and W-responsibilities run away;

Episode 7 Lawyer Purchased a Box of Cigars

Box of Twenty-six Cuban Cigars

A lawyer purchased a box of very rare and expensive cigars; then insured them, among other things, against fire. Within a month, having smoked his entire stockpile of these great cigars and without yet having made even his first premium payment on the policy, the lawyer filed a claim against the insurance company. In his claim, the lawyer stated that the cigars were lost in "a series of small fires." The insurance company refused to pay, citing the obvious reason that the man had consumed the cigars in the normal fashion. The lawyer sued. And won!

In delivering the ruling, the judge agreed with the insurance company that the claim was frivolous. Nevertheless, the judge stated that the lawyer held a policy from the company in which it had warranted that the cigars were insurable and also guaranteed that it would insure them against fire, without defining what is considered to be unacceptable and was obligated to pay the claim. Rather than endure a lengthy and costly appeal process, the insurance company accepted the ruling and paid $15,000 to the lawyer for the cigars lost in the 'fires.'

Has Justice been done? Just stay with me.

After the lawyer cashed his check, the insurance company had him arrested on 24 counts of arson! With his insurance claim and testimony from the previous case being used against him, the lawyer was convicted of intentionally burning his insured property and was sentenced to 24 months in jail and a $24,000 fine.

Now; has Justice been done?

Aristo: "Anybody can become angry; that is easy. But to be angry with the right person, to the right degree, at the right time, for the right purpose, and in the right way; that is not within everybody's power and it is not easy; and it is not easy to be Just. It requires character."

Alexander (a student of *Aristo*): "*Aristo*'s keen observations on the human and canine condition, alike, are profound. Anger results from being wronged or the perception of being wronged. Being able to dispassionately evaluate a 'wrong' is paradoxical; doable but it takes a lot of discipline and emotional intelligence. To untangle the Knot of Gordian by hand can cause a lot of frustration; so I did it with a single stroke of my sword – a show of discipline and emotional intelligence."

Aristo: "I am indeed for self-control but the judge would have done everyone a service if he were to raise the sword of Justice and cut the lawyer's claim into smithereens.

She would have served everyone better; maybe even served the greater good."

Plato: "When systems of Justice seem out of whack, it's because they are modeled incorrectly; they are not based on a foundation of ethics and they are executed by people who lack proper ethical understanding. The first step is to have a Just society, and a system of Justice as part of its ethical understanding."

Aristo: "I agree. Justice is one of the four cardinal virtues; and sometimes as the most important of the four."

Plato: "But the critical step is to make ethics the foundation of the system of Justice. Without ethical understanding; there can be no Justice. The idea of Justice occupies center stage both in ethics, and in legal and political philosophy. It is applicable to individual actions, to laws, and to public policies, and we think in each case that if they are unjust this is a strong, maybe even a conclusive, reason to reject them."

Kant: "Justice should be the first virtue of social institutions. We might debate which of these realms of practical philosophy has first claim on Justice: is it first and foremost a property of the law, for example, and only derivatively a property of individuals and other institutions?"

Alexander: The lawyer was unethical, conniving, and a shyster; yet, our laws did not permit me to slice him up with my sword. The insurance company having drafted an erroneous policy enabled the lawyer and then made up for it by using the law to level the playing field. Was it legal: by all means it was; was it ethical: I doubt it very much."

Rumi: "I hate cigar smoke. It gets in my eyes."

Rumi, Aristo, Alexander, Plato, and Kant: chanting:
"Hear, Hear!...
Hear, Hear!...
Hear, Hear!..."

As they disappear from the scene, they leave the judge behind with a nondescript expression on her face

About the Author

Ömer Akın, has been a registered, practicing architect in the state of Pennsylvania, USA, for nearly 40 years. He has been teaching in the School of Architecture at Carnegie Mellon University, since 1977 and was responsible for a required course on *Ethical Decision Making in Architecture* for three decades.

He authored six technical and textbooks that Amazon still offers: *Representation and Architecture; Psychology of Architectural Design; A Cartesian Approach to Design Rationality; Generative CAD Systems;* and *Embedded Commissioning of Building Systems*. The *Psychology of Architectural Design* has been a seminal title in the area of "design thinking" for over three decades.

A former colleague, Bharat Dave, wrote the following words about the *Cartesian Approach to Design Rationality:* "Anyone who thinks architectural design is a subjective and irrational activity undertaken by creative and self-absorbed architects in moody offices in sublime isolation should take note... This book brings together support from fields as diverse as sciences, philosophy, cognitive psychology, design computation, and others to argue that architectural design is (and ought to be) an objective and rational process...."

The publishers of *Embedded Commissioning of Building Systems* write: "[This book] provides an understanding of the underpinnings of embedded commissioning as the overarching building evaluation approach. [It] includes details on research findings in the areas of sensor networks, field tools and AR/AV methods, just-in-time technologies, and wearable computers."

Ömer Akin

Citations *and* Bibliography

Adams, Robert Merihew, 2006, *A Theory of Virtue*, New York: Oxford University Press.

Akın, Ö. (1978) "How do architects design?" in *Artificial Intelligence and Pattern Recognition in Computer-Aided Design* ed. by J. Latombe, North Holland, New York

Akın, Ö. (1986, 1989) *Psychology of Architectural Design* **Pion Limited, London**

Akın, Ö. (1988) "Expertise of the Architect" in *Expert Systems for Engineering Design* edited by Michael D. Rychener, Academic, New York, pp. 171-196

Akın, Ö. (1990) "Necessary conditions for design expertise and creativity" in *Design Studies* 11, 2, 107-113

Akın, Ö. (1993) "Architects' reasoning with structures and functions" in *Environment and Planning B: Planning and Design* 20 (1993) 273-294

Akın, Ö. (1994) "Creativity in Design" in *Performance Improvement Quarterly* 7,3 (1994) 9-21

Akın, Ö. and C. Akın (1996) "Frames of reference in architectural design: analyzing the hyper-acclamation (A-h-a-!)" *Design Studies* **17 (1996) 4, 341-361**

Akın, Ö. and C. T. Lin (1996) "Design protocol data and novel design decisions" in Analyzing Design Activity eds. N. Cross and K. Dorst, John Wiley and Sons, Chichester, West Sussex

Akın, Ö., N. Esin, and B. Uluoglu (1996) "Quality of architectural service in the project management process" in *Journal of Architectural Planning Research* 13, 1 (1996)63-90

Akın, Ö. and Ipek Özkaya (2007) "Tool Support For Computer-Aided Requirement Traceability in Architectural Design" in the *Journal of Automation in Construction*, 16, 674-684

Akın, Ö. (2017) *Applied Ethics Anecdotes; Narrated by a Cynocephalus*, Createspace, N. Charleston, SC.

Alazard, J. (1952) *Le Corbusier*, Milano

Alexander, C. (1964) *Notes on the Synthesis of Form* **Harvard University Press, Cambridge, MA**

Anderson, J R (1981) *Cognitive Skills and Their Acquisition* Hillsdale, New Jersey, Lawrence Erlbaum Associates

Annas, Julia, 1993, *The Morality of Happiness***, New York: Oxford University Press.**

Anscombe, F. J. and R. J. Auman (1963) "A definition of subjective probability" *Annals of Mathematical Statistics* **34, 199-205**

Architectural Forum "Slum Surgery in St. Louis" (April, 1951) pp. 128-136

Aristotle (1957) The *Physics* Harvard University Press, Loeb Classical Library, Cambridge, Massachusetts.

Aristotle (1990) *Nichomachean Ethics*, VI.4, 1140a in *Classics of Western Philosophy* by S. M. Cahn, Hackett Publishing, Indianapolis, Indiana.

Athanassoulis, Nafsika, 2000, "A Response to Harman: Virtue Ethics and Character Traits", *Proceedings of the Aristotelian Society* (New Series), 100: 215–21.

Audi, Robert, 2009, "Moral Virtue and Reasons for Action", *Philosophical Issues*, 19: 1–20.

Ayers, M. (1986) "Locke's Original Atomism" in *Rationalism, Empiricism and Idealism* by A. Kenny, Clarendon Press, Oxford

Badhwar, N.K., 1996, "The Limited Unity of Virtue", *Noûs*, 30: 306–29

Bailey, O., 2010, "What Knowledge is Necessary for Virtue?", *Journal of Ethics and Social Philosophy* 4 (2): 1–17

Barnes, L. B., C., R. Christensen, A. J. Hansen (1994) *Teaching and the Case Method*, Harvard Business School Press, Boston, Massachusetts

Battaly, H. (ed.), 2010, *Virtue and Vice, Moral and Epistemic*, a pair of special issues of Metaphilosophy, 41(1/2)

Baumol, W. J. (1972) *Economic Theory and Operations Analysis* Prentice-Hall, Englewood Cliffs, New Jersey.

Baxley, A. M., 2007, "The Price of Virtue", *Pacific Philosophical Quarterly*, 88: 403–23.

Beedle, L. C, (ed.) *Second Century of the Skyscraper*, Van Nostrand Reinhold Company, New York, 1988.

Besser-Jones, L., 2008, "Social Psychology, Moral Character and Moral Fallibility", *Philosophy and Phenomenological Research*, 76: 310–32

Brady, M. S., 2005, "The Value of the Virtues", *Philosophical Studies*, 125: 85–144

Broadbent, G. and A. Ward (1969) "Design Methods in Architecture" *Architectural Association* Paper Number 4, George Wittenborn Inc., New York.

Bruner, J. S., J. L. Goodnow, and G. A. Austin (1956) *A Study of Thinking* Wiley, New York

Cafaro, P. and R. D. Sandler (eds.), 2010, *Virtue Ethics and the Environment*, Dordrecht; New York: Springer.

Caroll, J. M. and J. C. Thomas and A. Malhotra (1978) "Presentation and representation in design problem solving" *British Journal of Psychology* 71, 143-153

Carr, D. and J. Steutel (eds.), 1999, *Virtue Ethics and Moral Education*, New York: Routledge.

Cavanaugh, S. J. (1984) "American Business Values," Chapter 5 in "Ethics in Business," Prentice Hall

Chappell, T. (ed.), 2006, *Values and Virtues*, Oxford: Oxford University Press.

Chase, W. G. and H. A. Simon (1973) "The mind's eye in chess" in *Visual Information Processing* edited by W.G. Chase, Academic Press, New York, pp. 215-282.

Checkoway, B. (1985) "Revitalizing an Urban Neighborhood: A St. Louis Case Study" ***The Metropolitan Midwest* Chicago: University of Illinois Press.**

Clarke, B., 2010, "Virtue and Disagreement", *Ethical Theory and Moral Practice*, 13: 273–91.

Cobb, H. (1986) *Architecture and the University: Walter Gropius Lecture*, Cambridge, MA: Harvard University, Graduate School of Design

Cohen M. S. (1993) " The naturalistic basis of decision biases" in Decision Making Actions: Models and Methods G. A. Klein, J. Orasanu, R Calderwood, C. E. Zsambok (eds.) Ablex Publishing Corporation, Norwood, NJ,

Collins, P. (1965) "Chapter 19: Rationalism" in *Changing Ideals in Modern Architecture* McGill-Queen's University Press, Montreal, pp. 198-217.

Coombs, C. H. (1964) *A Theory of Data* Wiley, New York.

Crisp, R. and Michael S. (eds.), 1997, *Virtue Ethics*, Oxford: Oxford University Press.

Cuff, D. *Architecture: The Story of Practice*, MIT Press, Cambridge, MA, 1992.

Curzer, H., 2010, "An Aristotelian Critique of the Traditional Family", *American Philosophical Quarterly:* 103–15.

Dalley, J. (1982) "Design creativity and the understanding of objects" *Design Studies* 3, 3, 133-137

deGroot, A. D. (1965) *Thought and Choice in Chess,* The Hague, Mouton.

deGroot, A. D. (1966) "Perception and memory versus thought: Some old ideas and recent findings" in *Problem Solving* edited by J Kleinmuntz, New York, John Wiley, pp. 19-50.

Delage, C. and N. Marda (1995) "Concept formation in a studio project" in *Educating Architects* edited by M. Pearce and M. Toy, New York: Academy Editions, pp. 65-67

DeMoss W. F. (1918) "Spenser's Twelve Moral Virtues According to Aristotle," *Modern Philology,* 16,. 1, 23-38

Dent, N.J.H., 1984, *The Moral Psychology of the Virtues*, Cambridge: Cambridge University Press.

DePaul, M. and L. Zagzebski (eds.), 2003, *Intellectual Virtue: Perspectives from Ethics and Epistemology*, New York: Oxford University press.

Doll, R., 2002. "Proof of Causality: Deduction from Epidemiological Observation". *Perspectives in Biology and Medicine.* **45 (4): 499–515.**
John M., 1998, "Persons, Situations and Virtue Ethics", *Noûs*, 32 (4): 504–30.
Driver, J., 2001, *Uneasy Virtue*, New York: Cambridge University Press.
Eckersley, M. (1988) "The form of design process: a protocol analysis study" *Design Studies* 9, 2, 86-84
Ericsson, K. A. and H. A. Simon (1993) *Protocol Analysis, Verbal Reports as Data* **Revised Edition, The MIT Press, Boston**
Feldman, I. and M.K. Lindell (1990) "On rationality" in I. Horowitz (ed.) *Recent Economic Thought: Organization and Decision Theory* **Kluwer Publishers, Boston**
Fitch, J. M. (1966) *American Building*, The Historical Forces that Shaped It second edition revised and enlarged The Riverside Press, Cambridge, MA, (first edition 1947).
Flemming, U. (1989) "More on the representation and generation of loosely packed arrangements of rectangles" *Environment and Planning B: Planning and Design* 16, 327- 359
Foot, P., 1978, *Virtues and Vices*, Oxford: Blackwell.
Frampton, K. (1987) *Modern Architecture, A Critical History* **second printing of the revised and enlarged edition, Thames and Hudson Ltd., London**
Freeman, P. A. and A. Newell (1971) "A model for functional reasoning in design" in *Proceedings of the Second International Joint Computer Conference on Artificial Intelligence* British Computer Society, 13 Mansfield atr, London W1M OBP, pp. 621-640.
Friedman, M., 2009, "Feminist Virtue Ethics, Happiness and Moral Luck", *Hypatia*, 24: 29–40
Gardiner, S. (ed.), 2005, *Virtue Ethics, Old and New*, Ithaca: Cornell University Press.

Gauthier D. (1986) *Morals by Agreement*, **Oxford University Press**
Geach, P., 1956, "Good and Evil," *Analysis*, 17: 33–42
Gerard, R. W. (1946) "The biological basis of imagination; with biological sketches" *Scientific Monthly* Vol. 62, pp. 477-499
Getzels, J. W. (1982) "Without questions, what would the answer be?" in *Question Framing and Response Consistency* by Robin M. Hogarth, San Francisco, Jossey-Bass Inc., Publishers, pp. 37-50.
Gewirth, A. (1984) *The Epistemology of Human Rights. Social Philosophy and Policy* **1 (02):1-.**
Gewirth, A. (1984) "Rational Basis of Professional Ethics" in *Current Problems of Professional Ethics*, **Symposium Proceedings, U of Nebraska, 1984**
Goor, A. (1974) "Problem Solving Processes of Creative and Non-creative Students" *Dissertation Abstracts* International University of North Carolina, 74, 3, 3517A
Gottfriedson, M. R. and D. M. Gottfriedson (1988) *Decision Making in Criminal Justice, Toward the Rational Exercise of Discretion* Plenum Press, New York, Second Edition.
Goumain, P. G. (1973) "Design methods and designer's methods" in *The Design Activity International Conference* Volume I, Printing Unit, University of Strathclyde, Glasgow, pp. 23.1-23.8.
Gowans, C. W., 2011, "Virtue Ethics and Moral Relativism", in Stephen D. Hales (ed.), *A Companion to Relativism*, New York: Oxford University Press, pp. 391–410.
Grayling A. C. (ed.) (1995) *Philosophy*, **Oxford University Press.**
Gregory, S., Ed. (1966) *The Design Method* Butterworth Inc., London.
Gropius, W. (1965) *The New Architecture and the Bauhaus* (paperback edition) The MIT Press, Cambridge, MA

Guilford, J P (1950) "Creativity" *American Psychology* Vol. 5, pp. 444-54.

Hacker-Wright, J., 2007, "Moral Status in Virtue Ethics", *Philosophy*, 82: 449–73

Halwani, R., 2003, *Virtuous Liaisons*, Chicago: Open Court.

Harman, G., 1999, "Moral Philosophy Meets Social Psychology: Virtue Ethics and the Fundamental Attribution Error", *Proceedings of the Aristotelian Society* (New Series), 119: 316–31.

Hayes, J. R. (1982) "Issues in protocol analysis" *Decision Making: An Interdisciplinary Inquiry* **Kent Publishing Company, Boston, MA, pp.61-63.**

Hillier, B., J. Musgrove, and P. O'Sullivan (1984) "Knowledge and design" in *Developments in Design Methodology* **ed. by Nigel Cross, John Wiley and Sons, Chichester, New York**

Hinman, L., *Ethics: A Pluralistic Approach to Moral Theory*, Third Edition Wadsworth, Belmont, CA, 2002

Hobhouse, C. (1950) *1851 and the Crystal Palace* John Murray, Albemarle Street, London

Hoffman, Alexander von, "Why They Built the Pruitt–Igoe Project" Joint Center for Housing Studies, Harvard University. [permanent dead link].

Hogarth, R. M. (ed.) (1982) *Question Framing and Response Consistency* Jossey-Bass Inc., San Francisco

Holmes, E (1878) *The Life of Mozart Including His Correspondence* **Chapman and Hall, pp. 211**

Horowitz, I. (1990) *Organization and Decision Theory* Kluwer Academic Publishers, Boston.

Hudson, S., 1986, *Human Character and Morality*, Boston: Routledge & Kegan Paul.

Hurka, T., 2001, *Virtue, Vice, and Value*, Oxford: Oxford University Press.

Hursthouse, R., 1990–1, "After Hume's Justice", *Proceedings of the Aristotelian Society*, 91: 229–45

Hursthouse, R., 1999, *On Virtue Ethics*, Oxford: Oxford University Press.
Jackendoff, R. (1983) *Semantics and Cognition* The MIT Press, Cambridge, MA.
Johnson, R. N., 2003, "Virtue and Right", *Ethics*, 133: 810–34
Kahneman, D. and A. Tversky (1979) "Prospect theory: an analysis of decision under risk" *Econometrica* **47, 263-91.**
Kamtekar, R., 2004, "Situationism and Virtue Ethics on the Content of Our Character", *Ethics*, 114: 458–91
Kant, I. (1958) *Critique of Pure Reason* translation and introduction by Norman Kemp Smith, University of Edinburgh, Abridged Edition, The Modern Library, New York.
Kawall, J., 2009, "In Defence of the Primacy of Virtues", *Journal of Ethics and Social Philosophy*, 3 (2): 1–21.
Keller, S., 2007, "Virtue Ethics is Self-Effacing", *Australasian Journal of Philosophy*, 85 (2): 221–32.
Kenny, A. (1986) *Rationalism Empiricism and Idealism* Oxford Press
Kolodner Janet 1993 *Case-Based Reasoning*, Morgan Kaufmann Publishers. New York
Kretschmer, E (1931) *The Psychology of Men of Genious* Kegan Paul and Harcourt, Brace.
Kristjánsson, K., 2008, "An Aristotelian Critique of Situationism", *Philosophy*, 83: 55–76
Kuhn, T. (1970) *The Structure of Scientific Revolutions* second edition, International Encyclopedia of Unified Science Volume 2, Number 2, University of Chicago Press, Chicago.
Landau, R. "Architecture, Ethics, and the Person" in M. Pollak, *The Education of the Architect*, The MIT Press, Cambridge, MA, 1997
Le Corbusier (1986) *Towards a New Architecture* translated from Vers Une Architecture by Frederick Etchelles, Dover Publications, Inc., New York

LeBar, M., 2009, "Virtue Ethics and Deontic Constraints", *Ethics*, 119: 642–71
Lee, W. (1971) *Decision Theory and Human Behavior* Wiley, New York
Levy, D. N. L. (1990) "How will chess programs beat Kasparov?" in *Computers Chess and Cognition* ed. by T. A. Marsland and J. Schaeffer, Springer-Verlag, New York.
Lindsay, P. H. and D. A. Norman (1972) *Human Information Processing* Academic Press, New York
Locke, J. (1986) *An Essay Concerning Human Understanding* ed. P. H. Nidditch, Oxford, 1975, XV, 5, quoted in "Locke and the ethics of belief" by J. A. Passmore in *Rationalism, Empiricism and Idealism* by A. Kenny, Clarendon Press, Oxford
MacIntyre, A., 1985, *After Virtue*, London: Duckworth, 2nd Edition.
Mackinder, M. and H. Marvin (1982) "Design decision making in architectural practice" *Research Paper 19*, Institute of Advanced Architectural Studies, University of York, The King's Manor, York, YO12EP, U.K.
Mackinnon, D, W, (1970) "The Personality Correlates of Creativity: A Study of American Architects" in *Creativity* edited by P E Vernon, Penguin Books Ltd., Harmondsworth, Middlesex, pp 289-311
Martinez, J., 2011, "Is Virtue Ethics Self-Effacing?", *Australasian Journal of Philosophy*, 89 (2): 277–88.
McAleer, S., 2007, "An Aristotelian Account of Virtue Ethics: An Essay in Moral Taxonomy", *Pacific Philosophical Quarterly*, 88: 308–25.
McDowell, J. (1979) "Virtue and Reason", *Monist*, 62: 331–50.
Meehan, Eugene J. (1975) *Public housing; Convention versus Reality*, Center for Urban Policy Research, Rutgers, the State University
Merritt, M., 2000, "Virtue Ethics and Situationist Personality Psychology", *Ethical Theory and Moral Practice*, 3: 365–83

Messent, D. (1997) *Opera House: Act One,* David Messent *Photography,* Sydney, Australia

Millar, C. J. (1986) *Frank Lloyd Wright Letters to Clients,* The California State University Press, Fresno, CA

Miller, G. A. (1956) "The magical number seven, plus or minus two" *Psychological Review* 63, 2

Miller, G. A., E. Galanter, and K. H. Pribram (1960) *Plans and the Structure of Behavior* Henry Holt, New York.

Mitchell, W. J. (1990) *The Logic of Architecture* The MIT Press, Cambridge, MA.

Mitchell, W. J., P. Steadman and R. S. Liggett (1976) "Synthesis and optimization of small rectangular floor plans" *Environment and Planning B: Planning and Design* 3, 1, 37-70.

Mogulescu, M. (1970) *Profit through Design* American Management Association, Inc

Montgomery, Roger (1985) "Pruitt–Igoe: Policy Failure or Societal Symptom". The Metropolitan Midwest Urbana, Chicago: University of Illinois Press.

Moore, G. T. (ed.) *Emerging Methods in Environmental Design and Planning* The MIT Press, Cambridge, Massachusetts, 1970.

Moore, H (1955) "Notes on Sculpture" in *The Creative Process* edited by B Ghiselin, New York, Mentor Books

Mudge, A. E. (1971) *Value Engineering: A Systematic Approach,* McGraw-Hill, New York

Murvin, H. L. *The Architect's Responsibilities,* **Library of Congress Catalogue Number 82-90109, 1982**

Nagel, E. and J. R. Newman (1958) *Goedel's Proof* Routledge & Kegan Paul Ltd., London.

Neumann, J. von and Morgenstern, O, *Theory of Games and Economic Behavior.* **Princeton, NJ. Princeton University Press, 1953.**

Newell, A. (1968) "On the analysis of human problem solving protocols" in *Calcul et Formalisation dans les Sciences de L'Homme* edited by J.C. Gardin and B. Jaulin, Centre National de la Recherche Scientifique, Paris.

Newell, A. (1970) "Heuristic programming: ill-structured problems" in *Progress in Operations Research* Volume 3, ed. by J. A. Arnofsky, John Wiley, New York, pp. 360-414.

Newell, A. and H. A. Simon (1972) *Human Problem Solving* **Prentice-Hall, Englewood Cliffs, New Jersey**

Newell, A., J. C. Shaw, and H. A. Simon (1958) "Elements of a theory of human problem solving" *Psychological Review* 65, 3

Newmarch, R (1906) *Life and Letters of Peter Ilich Tchaikovsky* John Lane, pp. 274-275.

Nussbaum, M. C., 1990, "Aristotelian Social Democracy", in R. Douglass, G. Mara, and H. Richardson (eds.), *Liberalism and the Good*, New York: Routledge, pp. 203–52.

Nussbaum, M. C., 2006, *Frontiers of Justice*, Cambridge, Mass.: Harvard University Press.

Penslar, R. L,. 1995. *Research Ethics: Cases and Materials.* Bloomington: Indiana University Press.

Peterson, C. R., and L. R. Beach (1968) "Man as an intuitive statistician" *Psychology Bulletin* **68, 29-46**

Pettigrove, G., 2011, "Is Virtue Ethics Self-Effacing?", *Journal of Ethics*, 15 (3): 191–207

Pevsner, N. (1949) *Pioneers of Modern Design* New York

Piaget, J. (1947) *The Psychology of Intelligence* translated from French by Malcolm Piercy, Routledge & Kegan Paul, London.

Poincarè, H (1962) *Science and Method* translated by F. Maitland, New York, Dover, p 51

Polya, G. (1973) *How to Solve It*, A New Aspect of Mathematical Method Princeton, New Jersey, Princeton University Press

Pratt, J. W., H. Raiffa, and R. Schlaifer (1964) "The foundations of decision under uncertainty: an elementary exposition" *Journal of American Statistical Association* 59, 353-343.

Prinz, J., 2009, "The Normativity Challenge: Cultural Psychology Provides the Real Threat to Virtue Ethics", *Journal of Ethics*, 13: 117–44.

Quine, W. V. O. (1987) *Quiddities: An Intermittently Philosophical Dictionary* The Belknap Press of Harvard University Press, Cambridge, MA.

Radford, A. and J. Gero (1986) *Design by Optimization in Architecture and Building* Van Nostrand Reinhold, New York

Rainwater, L. (2006) [1970]. *Behind Ghetto Walls: Black Families in a Federal Slum.* **Chicago: Aldine Transaction. ISBN 978-0-202-30907-1.**

Rawls, J. (1999) *A Theory of Justice*, Harvard University Press.

Reitman, W. R. (1964) "Heuristic decision procedures, open constraints and structure of ill-defined problems" in *Human Judgments and Optimality* **edited by M. W. Shelly and G. L. Bryan, John Wiley, New York, pp. 282-315**

Revesz, G. E. (1988) *Lambda-Calculus, Combinatorics and Functional Programming* Cambridge University Press, Cambridge.

Richards, W. (1988) *Natural Computation* The MIT Press, Cambridge, MA.

Ridley, A. (1998) *Beginning Bioethics*. New York: St. Martin's Press.

Rogers, C R (1970) "Towards a theory of creativity" in *Creativity* edited by P E Vernon, Penguin Books Ltd., Harmondsworth, Middlesex, England, pp. 137-152.

Rosenman, M., J. Gero, and R.E. Oxman (1992) "What is a case?" in *CAAD Futures '91 Computer Aided Architectural Design* – Education, Research, Application ed. By G. Schmitt, Wieweg, Wisbaden, Germany, pp. 285-300.

Rowe, P. (1987) *Design Thinking* The MIT Press, Cambridge, Massachusetts.
Ruskin, J. *The Seven Lamps of Architecture*, Straus, and Giroux, New York, 1981
Russell, D. C., 2008, "Agent-Based Virtue Ethics and the Fundamentality of Virtue", *American Philosophical Quarterly*, 45: 329–48
Saint, A. (1983) *The Image of the Architect* Yale University Press, New Haven
Sandler, R. (2007) *Character and Environment: A Virtue-Oriented Approach to Environmental Ethics*, New York: Columbia University Press.
Sarin, R. K. (1990) "Analytical Issues in Decision Methodology" in *Organization and Decision Theory* ed. by I. Horowitz, Kluwer Academic Publishers, Boston, pp. 13-63.
Savage, L.J. (1954) *The Foundations of Statistics* John Wiley and Sons, New York.
Schoemaker, P. J. H. (1980) *Experiments on Decisions Under Risk: The Expected Utility Hypothesis* Kluwer-Nijhoff Publishing, Boston.
Scruton, R. (1981) *From Descartes to Witgenstein, A Short History of Modern Philosophy* Routledge and Kegan Paul, London.
Simon, H. A. (1957) *Models of Man: Social and Rational,* Wiley, New York.
Simon, H. A. (1969) *The Sciences of the Artificial* The MIT Press, Cambridge MA.
Simon, H. A. (1970) "Style in design" in *Proceedings of the Environmental Design Research Association Conference* II Department of Architecture, Carnegie-Mellon University, Pittsburgh, PA, pp. 1-10.
Simon, H. A. (1973) "The structure of ill structured problems" in *Artificial Intelligence* 4, 181-201
Slote, Michael, 1993, "Virtue ethics and Democratic Values", *Journal of Social Philosophy*, 14: 5–37

Slovic, P. B. Fischhoff, and S. Lichtenstein (1977) "Behavioral Decision Theory" in *Annual Review of Psychology* 28, 1-39.

Solomon, D. (1988) "Internal Objections to Virtue Ethics", *Midwest Studies in Philosophy*, 13: 428–41, reprinted in Statman 1997.

Sreenivasan, G. (2002) "Errors about Errors: Virtue Theory and Trait Attribution", *Mind*, 111 (January): 47–68.

Statman, D. (ed.) (1997) *Virtue Ethics*, Edinburgh: Edinburgh University Press.

Statman, D. (1997) "Introduction" in *Virtue Ethics* edited by D. Statman, Georgetown University Press, Washington, D.C.

Stevens, G. (1990) The Reasoning Architect, *Mathematics and Science in Design* McGraw-Hill Publishing Co., New York.

Stichter, Matt. (2011) "Virtues, Skills, and Right Action", *Ethical Theory and Moral Practice*, 14: 73–86.

Stocker, M. (1976) "The Schizophrenia of Modern Ethical Theories", *Journal of Philosophy*, 14: 453–66

Svensson, F. (2010) "Virtue Ethics and the Search for an Account of Right Action", *Ethical Theory and Moral Practice*, 13: 255–71.

Swanton, C. (2003) *Virtue Ethics: A Pluralistic View*, Oxford: Oxford University Press.

Toker, F. (2004) *Fallingwater Rising*, Alfred A. Knopf

Tversky, A. (1969) "Intransitivity of preferences" *Psychological Review* 76, 31-48

Tversky, A. (1972) "Elimination by aspects: a theory of choice" *Psychological Review* 79, 281-99.

Tversky, A. and D. Kahneman (1974) "Judgments under uncertainty: heuristics and biases" *Science* 185, 1124-31.

Upton, C. (ed.), 2009, *Virtue Ethics and Moral Psychology*: The Situationism Debate, a pair of special issues of The Journal of Ethics, 13 (2/3).

Valery, P. (1947) *The living Thoughts of Descartes* David McKay Company, Washington Square, Philadelphia.

van Zyl, Liezl, 2009, "Agent-Based Virtue Ethics and the Problem of Action Guidance" *Journal of Moral Philosophy*, 6 (1): 50–69.
Venturi, R. (1966) *Complexity and Contradiction in Architecture* The Museum of Modern Art Papers on Architecture, published by The Museum of Modern Art, New York.
Vernon, P E (1970) "Introduction" in *Creativity* edited by P E Vernon, Penguin Books Ltd., Harmondsworth, Middlesex, England, pp. 9-16.
Viollet-le-Duc E. E. (1959) *Discourses on Architecture* **Grove Press, Inc., New York.**
Viollet-le-Duc E. E. (1987) *Lectures on Architecture* Dover Publications Inc., New York
Vitruvius, P. (1999) *Ten Books on Architecture* **translation by Ingrid D. Rowland New York: Cambridge University Press, 1999.**
Wason, P.C. and P. N. Johnson-Laird (1972) *Psychology of Reasoning, Structure and Content* Harvard University Press, Cambridge MA
Wasserman, B. P. J. Sullivan, G. Palermo (2000) *Ethics and the Practice of Architecture*, Wiley, New York
Watson, Gary, 1990, "On the Primacy of Character", in *Flanagan and Rorty*, pp. 449–83, reprinted in Statman, 1997.
Webb, E. J. (1966) *Unobtrusive Methods* Rand McNally, Chicago.
Whitehead, A. N. *Essays in Science and Philosophy*, New York: Philosophical Library, Inc., 1947.
Williams, B. 1985, *Ethics and the Limits of Philosophy***, Cambridge, Mass.: Harvard University Press.**
Zagzebski, L., 1996, *Virtues of the Mind*, New York: Cambridge University Press.

ENDNOTES

i   Also see the Encyclopedia of Creativity, Invention, Innovation, and Entrepreneurship
http://blog.entrepreneurthearts.com/2011/05/08/springer-encyclopedia-of-creativity-invention-innovation-and-entrepreneurship

ii   From Latin: Mos, meaning habit, custom, manner

iii   In Chapter 10, in the section titled Architectural Decision Making, we will discuss the emergence of the profession in the US.

iv   The Temple of Atena at the Athens Acropolis

v   Murvin, 1982, LCC number 82-90109

vi   Anonymous in Cuff, 1992, pp. 68

vii   M. Graves in Cuff, 1992, pp. 219

viii   Ibid.

ix   Michelangelo, Vasari 1963: v 304, in Cuff, 1992, pp. 72

x   Cuff, 1992, pp. 132

xi   Ibid.

xii   Cuff, 1992, pp. 115

xiii   Cuff, 1992, pp. 87

xiv   Vitruvius (II.i.1-3) in Smith, C. Architecture in the Culture of Early Humanism, Oxford Press, NY, 1992, p. 29

xv   Smith, pp. 47-51

xvi   Ruskin, 1981

xvii   Ruskin, 1981, p. 39

xviii   Landau, 1997, pp. 417-420

xix   Akin, O. "Introduction," class notes for Ethical Decision Making in Architecture, School of Architecture, Carnegie Mellon University, Spring 2004.

xx   Chapter 17 describes the Kansas City Hyatt case where the option of recalculating the joint details of the box beams carrying the suspended atrium bridges went unnoticed for a long time and lead to the tragic events of June 17,198

xxi   Heuristics is an area of research in cognitive psychology that has grown to a level of prominence, recently. It attempts to explain human cognitive behavior based on informal rules of thumb, or "pretty good rules" of Decision Making.

xxii   Herbert A Simon (1916-2001)

xxiii   First principles are relationships that represent immutable truths as defined in the natural sciences (Akin, A Cartesian Approach to Design Rationality, METU Press, Ankara, 2005, Chapter 1)

xxiv   Schoemaker, 1980, p. 2

xxv   Slovic, 1977, p. 29

xxvi   Lee, 1971, p. 5

xxvii   Feldman, I. and M.K. Lindell (1990)

xxviii   The vN-MT models the world of decisions through a set of outcomes, called X, and the set of probability distributions on X, called P. Given two possible payoff schemes, one, called p, with outcomes X' and probabilities P'; and the other, called q, with outcomes X" and probabilities P". With these assumptions, mathematically expressible axioms can be defined. These axioms articulate the First Principles of Economic Decision Making.

xxix   Schoemaker, 1980, p. 27

xxx   Schoemaker, 1980, p. 33
xxxi   Lindsay and Norman, 1972
xxxii   Miller, 1956
xxxiii Newell, 1972
xxxiv   Schoemaker, 1980, pp. 36-37
xxxv   Schoemaker, 1980, pp. 36-37
xxxvi   Tversky, 1974
xxxvii The word paradigm is used here in the sense that Thomas Kuhn has used it in The Structure of Scientific Revolutions (1962).
xxxviii In Chapter 10, we will elaborate this process, attempting to map some of the general observations about Decision Making into the specific domain of architecture through a specific case study: the Sydney Opera House.
xxxix   See the Encyclopedia of Creativity, Invention, Innovation, and Entrepreneurship
        http://blog.entrepreneurthearts.com/2011/05/08/springer-encyclopedia-of-creativity-invention-innovation-and-entrepreneurship
xl   Given 9 dots, arranged in a square layout, the challenge is to draw four straight lines which go through the middle of all of the dots without taking the pencil off the paper.
xli   http://www.brainstorming.co.uk/puzzles/ninedotsnj.html
xlii   Meaning "a building's elevation" view
xliii   Protocol Analysis, Revised Edition Verbal Reports as Data By K. Anders Ericsson and Herbert A. Simo, The MIT Press ,Boston, MA, 1993

xliv See Akin, O., in *Encyclopedia of Creativity, Invention, Innovation and Entrepreneurship*, Editor-in-chief: Carayannis, Elias G. 2013, http://www.springer.com/gp/book/9781461438571

xlv The characteristic spirit of a culture, era, or community as manifested in its beliefs and aspirations.

xlvi Messent (1997)

xlvii Ibid.

xlviii Ibid.

xlix Akin, O. "Value Based Design," class notes for Value Based Design in Architecture, School of Architecture, Carnegie Mellon University, Spring 2012

l ethos= "the characteristic spirit of a culture, era, or community as manifested in its beliefs and aspirations"

li *Protocol Analysis, Revised Edition Verbal Reports as Data* By K. Anders Ericsson and Herbert A. Simon, The MIT Press, Boston, 1993

lii Pfeiffer in Millar, 1986, p. 82

liii Ibid.

liv *Fallingwater: A Conversation with Edgar Kaufmann Jr.* (1994) 57min | Documentary; Director: Kenneth Love; http://www.imdb.com/title/tt0137509/?ref_=nv_sr_2

lv Pfeiffer in Millar, 1986, p. 83

lvi In 1963, Edgar Kaufmann, jr. donated and entrusted Fallingwater and the surrounding 1,543 acres of land to the Western Pennsylvania Conservancy.

lvii The California State University Press, Fresno, CA (1986)

lviii Millar, 1986, pp. 91-92

lix	Op.cit. p. 93
lx	Ibid.
lxi	Ibid.
lxii	Op.cit. p. 96
lxiii	Ibid.
lxiv	Op.cit. pp. 97-98
lxv	Op.cit. pp. 98-99
lxvi	Op.cit. pp. 102-103
lxvii	Op.cit. pp. 103-104
lxviii	An unrealized project designed by the French-Swiss architect Le Corbusier in 1930
lxix	Voices: Pruitt-Igoe, http://cb13.raimistdesign.com/wp-content/uploads/2013/09/Voices-pruitt-igoe.pdf
lxx	Public Housing Policy (New Brunswick: Center for Urban Policy Research, Rutgers-The State University, 1975), pp. 64-65
lxxi	Daniel Stokols, "The Experience of Crowding in Primary and Secondary Environments," Environment and Behavior, 8 (March, 1976), 49-86
lxxii	Akin, O. "Introduction," class notes for Ethical Decision Making in Architecture, School of Architecture, Carnegie Mellon University, Spring 2004.
lxxiii	Akin and Akin, 1998
lxxiv	https://en.wikipedia.org/wiki/James_Gallier
lxxv	The first three of these correspond to Vitruvius' famous triple: Firmness, Commodity and Delight
lxxvi	These formal methods will be reviewed in the following Chapters of this Part.

lxxvii   Simon, 1972
lxxviii   Simon, 1973
lxxix   Ibid.
lxxx   Le Corbusier, 1976, pp. 153
lxxxi   Kant, 1958, p.41
lxxxii   Frampton, 1987, p. 9
lxxxiii   Vitruvius, 1906, Book I, Chapter 12, Item 2
lxxxiv   Alexander, 1964, p. 8
lxxxv   Viollet-le-Duc, 1987, pp 449-450
lxxxvi   Simon, 1969
lxxxvii   See Episode 4 for an ethics discussion of this hypothetical case
lxxxviii Lecture by Peter Madsen, Director of the Applied Ethics Center at Carnegie Mellon University, in Ethical Decision Making class, Fall 2003
lxxxix   Peter Madsen is an award-winning educator, trainer, writer and producer of educational media in the field of applied ethics. He teaches courses in business, professional, computer, and environmental ethics in CMU's Department of Philosophy. Madsen also teaches graduate management ethics and ethics and public policy courses in CMU's Heinz College and at GESPIA, at the University of Pittsburgh. He is Visiting Professor at the American University of Paris where he teaches International Business Ethics.
xc   Developed by International Alliance for Interoperability (IAI)
xci   https://en.wikipedia.org/wiki/Powergaming
xcii   "Project Management for Construction: Fundamental Concepts for Owners, Engineers, Architects and Builders," Chris

Hendrickson, Department of Civil and Environmental Engineering, Carnegie Mellon University, Pittsburgh, PA 15213 First Edition originally printed by Prentice Hall, ISBN 0-13-731266-0, 1989 with co-author Tung Au.

xciii Project Management Institute, A Guide to the Project Management Body of Knowledge, Newtown Square, Pennsylvania, 2000.

xciv Miller, G., Information Processing Theory.

xcv Akin, O. (1993) "An empirical view of the project management process," Proceedings of the First International Conference on The Management of Information Technology Conference, Singapore, 17-20 August, with N. Esin and B. Uluoglu

xcvi By "formal" we mean the presence of mathematical formulations of all of the three ingredients and absence of "incomputable" domains of optimality.

xcvii It is conceivable that one can represent a problem as an optimization problem without using mathematical notation. In such cases the standard techniques of evaluation do not apply and there is little guarantee that this kind of formalization is of any use.

xcviii Akin, et.al., 1992

xcix NBS BUILDING SCIENCE SERIES 143: Investigation of the Kansas City Hyatt Regency Walkways Collapse. http://fire.nist.gov/bfrlpubs/build82/PDF/b82002.pdf

c Ibid.

ci https://ws680.nist.gov/publication/get_pdf.cfm?pub_id=908286

cii NBS BUILDING SCIENCE SERIES 143: Investigation of the Kansas City Hyatt Regency Walkways Collapse. http://fire.nist.gov/bfrlpubs/build82/PDF/b82002.pdf.

ciii	Ibid.
civ	Ibid.
cv	Ibid.
cvi	Ibid.
cvii	Ibid.
cviii	Ibid.
cix	Ibid.
cx	from Encyclopedia.com:https://www.encyclopedia.com /humanities/ encyclopedias-almanacs-transcripts-and-maps/applied-ethics
cxi	https://www.theguardian.com/sustainable-business/2016/jan/11/five-sustainability-stories-define-next-decade-china-antibiotics-water
cxii	Ma Jun is a Chinese environmentalist, environmental consultant, and journalist. He is a director of the Institute of Public & Environmental Affairs (IPE)
cxiii	a concept meaning non-action or non-doing
cxiv	from Encyclopedia.com:https://www.encyclopedia.com /humanities/ encyclopedias-almanacs-transcripts-and-maps/applied-ethics.
cxv	Kritik der reinen Vernunft, 1781
cxvi	https://www.theguardian.com/sustainable-business/2016/jan/11/five-sustainability-stories-define-next-decade-china-antibiotics-water
cxvii	from Encyclopedia.com:https://www.encyclopedia.com /humanities/ encyclopedias-almanacs-transcripts-and-maps/applied-ethics

cxviii *from Encyclopedia.com:https://www.encyclopedia.com /humanities/ encyclopedias-almanacs-transcripts-and-maps/applied-ethics.*

Ethical Decision Making in Architecture ● Ömer Akin

www.ingramcontent.com/pod-product-compliance
Lightning Source LLC
Chambersburg PA
CBHW020847090426
42736CB00008B/269